THE MEANING IN THE MIRACLES

The Meaning in the Miracles

JEFFREY JOHN

William B. Eerdmans Publishing Company
Grand Rapids, Michigan / Cambridge, U.K.

First published 2001 in the United Kingdom by
Canterbury Press, Norwich

This edition published 2004 in the United States of America by
Wm. B. Eerdmans Publishing Co.
255 Jefferson Ave. S.E., Grand Rapids, Michigan 49503 /
P.O. Box 163, Cambridge CB3 9PU U.K.
www.eerdmans.com

Printed in the United States of America

09 08 07 06 05 04   7 6 5 4 3 2 1

ISBN 0-8028-2794-2

Contents

Foreword

People are sometimes a bit panicked by biblical scholarship; they look at a commentary and think, 'They have taken away my Lord and I do not know where they have laid him'. What is so welcome about Jeffrey John's book is that he shows as abundantly as anyone could wish how sensitive scholarship opens up unexpected depths and joys in reading the Bible.

He does not begin from a position sceptical of miracles as such, but he quite rightly encourages us to ask, 'Why is this story told like this?' The gospel writers are not seeking to provoke simply an open-mouthed amazement; they want to prompt us to ask, 'What sort of changes does Jesus bring to the world and to my experience of it?' The result is a book that ranges widely and raises all sorts of questions about Christian discipleship and Christian theology. It is sometimes startling, often very moving, never dull. It puts again and again the question of whether and how I or we want to be healed. And the additional material by way of prayer and reflection at the end of each chapter is always excellent.

Jeffrey John brings to his task a full professional scholarly equipment, but also an outstanding record as a pastor, preacher and teacher in many different contexts. He is both a sensitive and a challenging guide to reading the Gospels afresh, and I know that this book will be for many a real stimulus to grow in faith and trust in the One whose 'works of power' were always a means of announcing the good news of his transforming love.

ROWAN WILLIAMS
November 2001

Acknowledgements

Every effort has been made by the author and publishers to contact the owners of copyright material. The publishers would be grateful to be informed of any omissions so that suitable acknowledgements can be made in any further reprints.

Pages 1–3 are adapted from 'Making Sense of Scripture' by Jeffrey John in *Living Tradtion*, edited by Jeffrey John, published and copyright 1992 by Darton, Longman and Todd Ltd and used by permission of the publishers.

Two prayers of Eric Abbott (pages 97, 165) are reprinted with permission from Forward Movement Publications, Cincinnati, Ohio, USA.

Edwin Markham's poem 'Outwitted' (page 33) is reproduced by permission of Harper Collins, Inc., New York.

Quotations by Henry Agar (page 126) and William Norman Ewer (page 114) are taken from *The Oxford Dictionary of Quotations* (4th edition 1992) and are used by permission of the Oxford University Press.

A prayer from a 'Rite for Blessing a Same-Sex Partnership' (page 165), taken from *Daring to Speak Love's Name*, edited by Elizabeth Stuart, 1992, is quoted by permission of the author, Jim Cotter, and the publishers, Hamish Hamilton.

'The Kingdom' by R. S. Thomas (page 142) is reproduced by permission of the Orion Publishing Group from *R. S. Thomas: Collected Poems 1949–1990*, published by Phoenix, 1995.

Four prayers (pages 109, 110, 165, 213), taken from *Women Included: A Book of Services and Prayers* by The St Hilda Community, 1991, are printed by permission of the publishers, SPCK.

The poems 'Lazarus to Christ' and 'Christ to Lazarus' (pages 224–5) are quoted from *The Collected Poems of David Constantine*, 1991 by permission of the publishers, Bloodaxe Books.

Translations of prayers from St Augustine of Hippo (page 82), Pope John XXIII (page 201) and the Jewish New Year Liturgy (page 117) are quoted from *The Oxford Book of Prayer*, ed. G. Appleton, 1985 and are quoted by permission of the publishers, Oxford University Press.

Crossroad Publishing, New York, to quote three poems of Miriam Therese Winter (pages 108, 213, 226), published in *Woman Word*, 1990, permission sought.

Curtis Brown Ltd, New York, to quote the translation of Alcuin's prayer on page 83, taken from *More Latin Lyrics* by Helen Waddell, ed. F. Corrigan, published by Norton, 1976, permission sought.

The Meaning in the Miracles

Missing the Point: Mr Davies and Miss Tomkins

At school we had two Religious Education teachers – they were referred to as 'Scripture teachers' at the time – called Mr Davies and Miss Tomkins. They were bewilderingly different in their approach to their subject. Mr Davies was an old-fashioned Welsh Nonconformist, a part-time minister in the local chapel. For Mr Davies his religion was his Bible and his Bible his religion. He believed his Bible in its plainest, most literal sense; had they only appeared in its pages, he would have believed in leprechauns, King Arthur and Father Christmas too. If we ever attempted to challenge Mr Davies's belief using archaeology, or the evidence for evolution, or by pointing out inconsistencies within Scripture itself, the response was always the same: 'My boy, that is just human pride, and human pride must not challenge the Word of God.' So arguing with Mr Davies was really rather a waste of time. Still, at least you knew where you stood.

Miss Tomkins was a different kettle of fish. She was an Anglican, and had 'Modern Views'. She had read modern books by modern theologians such as Bishop John Robinson, and these books had inflamed her with the idea that religion had to be made 'relevant to the young people of today'. Miss Tomkins's main method of being relevant was to dismiss anything that sounded supernatural as being 'primitive' and 'unscientific'. Her great speciality was demolishing miracles. If Mr Davies told us about the parting of the waters at the Red Sea, Miss Tomkins would tell us it was all to do with winds and tides and sandbanks, as if you could walk through the Red Sea any old time. If it was Moses' stick turning into a snake in front of Pharaoh, Miss Tomkins would tell us that snakes like that are two a penny in Egypt, and look just like sticks when they are frightened. When we came to the raising of Lazarus, she told us about cataleptic fits, which make people seem to be dead when they are not. And whenever it was a question of Jesus healing the sick, it was 'psychosomatic', she said. Miss Tomkins loved the word 'psychosomatic'. Indeed, if Miss Tomkins was right, the incidence of psychosomatic deafness, dumbness, blindness and leprosy in first-century Palestine was a miracle in itself!

I recall these two characters here because they usefully sum up the two standard approaches – to Scripture in general and to the miracles in particular – that are regularly encountered in schools and churches. Mr Davies embodies what might be called the literalist or fundamentalist approach. For Mr Davies everything in Scripture was to be taken at its plainest level of meaning, and must have happened exactly as it said. If one asked Mr Davies about the meaning of a particular miracle story, he would generally answer that the point was to prove the supernatural nature of Jesus. 'Well, it goes to show that Jesus is God, doesn't it?' he would say. 'After all, God can do what he likes.' This meant that for Mr Davies, doubting that a miracle story happened exactly as it said in the Gospels was tantamount to doubting the divinity of Christ. Compassion came into it too, at least in the healing miracles. But essentially the miracles were about evidence, a demonstration of divine power.

Miss Tomkins, by contrast, was not concerned with defending the divinity of Christ or the literal truth of Scripture. Miss Tomkins's was the *reductionist* approach: she wanted to reduce the miraculous element to something that could be readily grasped in this-worldly terms. Most of her explanations were naturalistic – 'demythologizing' in the most obvious sense. So, for example, when Jesus walked on the lake, there were convenient stepping stones just under the surface of the water – the disciples merely *thought* Jesus walked on the water, and this mistake was handed on in the tradition. The calming of the storm was a convenient coincidence. So were the shoals of fish that happened along just as Jesus told the disciples to cast their net. The changing of the water to wine at Cana was a practical joke of just the kind that guests perform at wedding receptions. When Miss Tomkins's explanations were not naturalistic, they were moralistic. When Jesus fed the five thousand, what *really* happened (she said) was that Jesus and the disciples shared out their own loaves and fishes just with the people nearest them; but then others, seeing this splendid example of unselfishness, were inspired to share what they had too, and so there was enough to go round everyone. 'The *real* miracle,' said Miss Tomkins, 'is when everyone discovers the joy of caring and sharing with others.' Edifying as this was, it did not strike us as especially miraculous – or even very interesting.

Mr Davies's literalism and Miss Tomkins's reductionism may look like diametrically opposite approaches, but they are not as different as they appear at first sight. Both were treating the miracle stories in a naively historical way, as if they were straightforward descriptions of what happened, or at least of what appeared to happen. The only difference was that Miss Tomkins wanted to look for this-worldly explanations of the apparent happening, while Mr Davies was more than satisfied with the supernatural one. Both assumed that the most – indeed the only – interesting thing about the miracles was the question of what did or did not *happen*. While they focused so narrowly on this unanswerable and therefore ultimately fruitless and boring question, they missed the point. The real nature and purpose of the Gospel miracles, and the depths and dimensions of meaning which they are written to convey, passed both of them – and therefore us – by completely.[1]

The Inside Meaning

St Augustine, in the fourth century, was already complaining that hearers of the Gospel miracles habitually got stuck on the 'wonder' element and on speculating whether such a thing could possibly have occurred; in doing so, he felt, they often missed the kernel for the shell:

> Let us ask the miracles themselves what they tell us about Christ, for they have a tongue of their own, if it can only be understood. Because Christ is the Word of God, all the acts of the Word become words to us. The miracle which we admire on the outside also has something inside which must be understood. If we see a piece of beautiful handwriting, we are not satisfied simply to note that the letters are formed evenly, equally and elegantly: we also want to know the meaning the letters convey. In the same way a miracle is not like a picture, something merely to look at and admire, and to be left at that. It is much more

like a piece of writing which we must learn to read and understand.[2]

Let us take the story of Jesus feeding the five thousand as an example of how to 'read the language' of miracle. Far from seeing it, as Mr Davies did, as a straightforward demonstration of divine power, or as Miss Tomkins did, as a moral lesson about caring and sharing, in order to 'read' this miracle accurately we first have to appreciate that, whatever history may lie behind it, this story in its present form is a literary creation with a theological purpose. Perhaps its most obvious theological aim is to tell us that Jesus is a new Moses. Even a modern reader with a sketchy knowledge of the Old Testament is likely to remember that Moses had done something similar with the manna in the desert, and closer examination reveals more detailed points of comparison. Like Moses, Jesus crosses the water into the desert, sits the people down in companies and feeds them with miraculous bread from heaven in such abundance that there are basketfuls left over. Much less obviously, because the relevant Old Testament story is less well known, Jesus' actions also recall Elisha. Some of the details of the story are clearly taken from an incident in 2 Kings 4 when Elisha takes an army of men into the desert and feeds them miraculously with a few loaves. Taking Elisha and Moses together, the story seems to be telling us in an allusive way that in recapitulating what Moses did Jesus fulfils the Law, and in recapitulating Elisha he fulfils the Prophets. The same idea enters into the Transfiguration story, where we see Moses and Elijah testifying to Jesus as the Messiah. Like the Transfiguration, this miracle is intended to teach us, in picture-story form, that Jesus is truly the one whom the Law and the Prophets foretold.

But there is much more. In Mark's and Matthew's Gospels the feeding of the five thousand is followed by an almost identical miracle two chapters further on (Matthew 15, 16 and Mark 6, 8). Jesus does the same thing again, but with different numbers of loaves, people and fishes. These numbers are clearly very significant, because in Mark's Gospel Jesus questions the disciples about them, and condemns their stupidity when (as so often in Mark) they fail to understand. Evidently the numbers are intended to be symbolic: we are probably meant to understand that those in the first miracle point to a Jewish context, and those in the second to a Gentile one. The two stories are therefore a sort of prefiguring of the two-stage preaching of the gospel, 'first to the Jew, then to the Greek'. The bread symbolizes the Word of God – a standard association in Jewish thinking, deriving from a reference to the manna story in Deuteronomy, which ends with the warning, 'you shall not live by bread alone but by every word that proceeds from the mouth of God'.[3] At the same time the bread also has a sacramental reference. The words and actions of Jesus over the bread are exactly the same as at the Last Supper, and the association with the Exodus events, and even Mark's mention that the grass was green, point to a Passover setting and thus to the new Christian Passover: the Eucharist.

Even this (as we shall see when we come to it in detail) does not exhaust the miracle's extraordinary complex of allusions, but enough has been said for the moment to point to the different levels of meaning which are conveyed by the story. These meanings are christological (that is, the miracle tells us something about Jesus' nature and identity); typological (because it relates Jesus to two comparable 'types' or figures of the religious past); eschatological (meaning that it relates to the 'end time', since it presents Jesus as the ultimate fulfilment of a tradition, and also prefigures the idea of the heavenly meal); symbolic (in its use of numbers, for example); and sacramental (in its reference to the Eucharist). All these dimensions of meaning were important to the Gospel writers and are still important to us – but they are regularly missed in the 'standard' approach to miracles, which is still the approach of too many school lessons, sermons and Bible studies.

The feeding of the five thousand, like many other Gospel miracles, has the literary character of a short *haggadah*. It is important to remember that the Gospel writers were Jews (with the possible exception of Luke), they were steeped in Old Testament Scripture, and they derived their literary and theological conventions from their Jewish antecedents. *Haggadah* (meaning 'narrative') is a creative genre of Jewish theological writing, which starts from scriptural texts as a base (as this miracle starts from the Moses and Elisha stories) but weaves upon it very freely, using threads of prophecy-fulfilment, symbolism, typology, allegory or numerology to create a new story which reapplies the truths, hopes, patterns and meanings of the scriptural past to the present. The best examples of Christian *haggadoth* in the New Testament are the birth and infancy narratives in Matthew's and Luke's Gospels, which are composed almost entirely of Old Testament themes and references, made into two new stories to illuminate the meaning of Christ's birth. This method of composition is most obviously seen in the longer 'set-piece' miracles – for example, the calming of the storm and the healing of the Gerasene demoniac, which together seem to be a 'double fulfilment story' on the base of Psalm 65:7 ('You, O Lord, still the roaring of the waves and the madness of the Gentiles') –

but a similar, literary-theological purpose and method underlies them all.

This means that most often the key to unlocking the theological meaning of a miracle story will lie in the Old Testament, and it is partly lack of knowledge of the Old Testament that makes the process less natural to us today. When reading the Gospels, and the miracle stories in particular, it is always enlightening to follow up cross-references in a good reference Bible, and better still to read the Gospels alongside a good scholarly commentary. Without this guidance the chances are the modern reader will miss the point – or more often a number of points. Of course there is a risk in going overboard in digging out scriptural allusions, and there are plenty of instances in patristic writing in particular of taking allegorical interpretation too far: St Augustine himself does so when he identifies the two fish in the feeding of the five thousand as Joshua and Zerubbabel, the priestly and princely rulers of Israel at the end of the exile! Ours, however, is much more likely to be the opposite fault, the one for which Jesus criticizes the disciples – of failing to see the allusions that really are intended, and without which the full meaning cannot be grasped.

Reading in Context: Including the Excluded

As well as understanding the context of the miracles in terms of the scriptural background and the literary conventions that helped shaped them, it is equally crucial to understand them in their own religious, historical, social and political context (meaning both the context of Jesus himself in which the miracle is set, and the context of the evangelist, which must be carefully distinguished). Take, for example, the healing of the woman with a haemorrhage

(Mark 5:25–34; Matthew 9:20–22; Luke 8:43–48). This miracle may be, and usually is, interpreted purely at the level of the story itself. It is a good story. The portrayal of a woman who had spent all her wealth on useless doctors; her terror as she creeps up to touch Jesus' cloak; the confused press of the crowd around them; Jesus' sharp question 'Who touched me?' as he senses the healing power flowing from him; the bemused response of the disciples; the woman's trembling admission; and finally the marvellous words of release and liberation, 'your faith has saved you' – all this makes it a peculiarly dramatic and poignant tale. But we will fail to understand its real point unless we realize the implications of the woman's sickness for herself and women in general.

In the Judaism of Jesus' time the concept of religious 'purity', one's labelling as 'clean' or 'unclean', was a marker of social and religious inclusion or exclusion. The nature of the woman's illness – a constant flow of blood – made her continually 'non-kosher', a social and a religious outcast; and she had suffered it continually for twelve years. The strength of the menstrual taboo, and the belief that the 'uncleanness' was contagious, meant that for a woman to touch a man, let alone a rabbi, during her period was a sternly punishable offence. Hence the woman's terror in approaching to touch Jesus. This taboo, of which every woman of childbearing age was reminded each month, contributed powerfully to the generally negative assessment of women in first-century Judaism: menstruation, like the pangs of childbirth, was seen literally as the sign of God's curse on woman for having led Adam into sin.

If we stay at the level of the story, the level of 'what happened' to the individual woman, we miss the extraordinary, world-changing meaning of what Jesus did. Certainly we see a moving example of Jesus' compassion in releasing a poor woman who had suffered exceptionally for many years, and that is marvellous enough. But this miracle is 'about' something of infinitely greater significance than the story of one woman. *We are shown Jesus overturning the menstrual taboo which subjugated and oppressed women – a taboo that still contributes today to the oppression of women in many parts of the world, and indeed in some parts of the Church.* The implication of this miracle is nothing less than revolutionary for half the human race, but it is still often passed over as if it were merely one more story about Jesus' healing compassion. Read properly, it challenges the Church to assess its own treatment of women today as powerfully as Jesus challenged the gynophobic conventions of his own time.

A similar point can be made about most, if not all, of the healing miracles. They seem to have been deliberately selected by the evangelists to show Jesus healing at least one of every category of persons who, according to the purity laws of Jesus' society, were specifically excluded and labelled unclean, or who were set at varying degrees of distance from worship in the inner temple. The list of those who suffered some degree of taboo and exclusion contains menstruating women, lepers, Samaritans, Gentiles, tax-collectors, homosexuals, prostitutes, adulteresses, women in general, children, people with withered limbs, the deaf, the dumb, the blind, the lame and the dead. At least one representative from each of these categories is a subject of Jesus' healing in the miracle stories. (The inclusion of someone in the homosexual category is debatable, but we shall see that there is good reason to believe that the story of the centurion and his servant would have been viewed under this heading.)

Each of these healings is, of course, a demonstration of Jesus' healing power and compassion for the individual, but that is not the main point. Uppermost in the evangelist's mind – and far more relevant to us – is the miracle's universal significance: the overturning of social and religious barriers; the abolition of taboos; and Jesus' declaration of God's love and compassion for everyone, expressed in the systematic inclusion of each class of the previously excluded or marginalized. It is worth noticing that very often these healing miracles lay emphasis on Jesus' *touching* the sufferer, precisely because the impurity that was supposedly involved in their disorder or sin was conceived literally as a contagion that might be passed on to others, making them equally 'unclean'. Jesus summarily dismisses both the quarantine rules and the taboo: the untouchables are the ones he positively goes out of his way to touch, embrace and include in his kingdom. He has come for the 'sick', not the 'well'; though as it turns out, the 'sick' are nearer salvation already since they know their need of it, while the 'well', seeing no need of it, shut it out. As we consider the meaning of these miracles for today, the question repeatedly poses itself: how far has the Church seen or wanted to see the implications of this systematic, subversive, highly risky inclusivism on Jesus' part, and preferred instead to create and cling to its own taboos?

Principalities and Powers

The first miracle that Jesus performs in Mark's Gospel is the exorcism of a demon-possessed man in the Capernaum synagogue (Mark 1:23–28). The crowd had already been astonished at Jesus' teaching, 'for he taught them as one who had authority, and not as the scribes'.[4] But then Jesus' authority is confirmed in a different way, when the demoniac shouts, 'What have you to do with us, Jesus of Nazareth? We know who you are. The Holy One of God!' After Jesus has cast out the demons, the crowd, who are slower than the demons to draw the obvious conclusion, exclaim, 'What is this? With authority he commands even the unclean spirits, and they obey him!' Within the drama of the gradual unfolding of Jesus' identity which is common to the Synoptic Gospels, one of the functions of the demonic powers is to demonstrate Jesus' real identity from the outset, while others, including his own disciples, remain blind to the implications of both his teaching and his miracles.

But possession by demonic forces is not always as obvious as in the case of the demoniac. From the Gospel writers' point of view, the whole world is in the grip of fallen powers, and their work is everywhere to be seen. All sickness, sin and disorder derive from their rule, not only explicitly 'supernatural' phenomena. So, for example, when Jesus heals a crippled woman, she is described as having been *bound by Satan* these eighteen years.[5] More oddly from a modern viewpoint, even natural forces may be viewed as driven by the same disordered, demonic power. When Jesus calms the storm in Mark's Gospel, the Greek text shows that he addresses it in exactly the same personal terms in which he addresses the demoniac, using language one might use to a mad dog: 'Be muzzled, cur!'[6] The sea had long been regarded in Hebrew tradition as the 'chaos' of the creation story: a natural home of sea-monsters and demonic forces hostile to God, which only he could subdue. So when Jesus walks on the water we are meant to recall that, according to the Psalms, Isaiah and Job, it is *God alone* 'who makes a way through the sea, a path through the mighty waters'. Here Mr Davies would be right: the purpose of this miracle really is to reveal the divinity of Jesus. And to confirm it, hidden in the greeting of Jesus to the terrified disciples in the boat is a revelation of the name of Yahweh himself: 'Fear not: I AM' (Mark 6:47-51). (Alas, this is visible only in the Greek. English translations usually have 'It is I', which misses the point.)

In the Synoptic Gospels especially, Jesus is presented as the one who bears God's unique authority and power to drive down the usurped authority of the demons. He is the 'Stronger One' promised in Isaiah who can defeat Satan's temptations and bind his powers;[7] and in the miracles we are meant to see the force of God's kingly rule driving back the frontiers of darkness and reclaiming God's creation for himself. But because one of the functions of evil is to blind human beings to the truth, most often this evidence for Jesus' true nature is missed or misunderstood. Even the disciples are slow enough to grasp it. But it is a measure of the depth of the Pharisees' depravity that, seeing Jesus' miracles and the manifest good produced by his healing power, they still wilfully attribute it to Satan, thus turning good and evil upside down and committing the 'unpardonable sin' against the Spirit.[8] So almost from the outset they become the main earthly manifestation of the evil powers that drive Jesus to the cross.

How are we meant to understand these demonic powers in the Gospels? Here too it is important to avoid the twin pitfalls of literalism and reductionism. We are not required to believe in the existence of fork-tailed demons, nor even, necessarily, in the powers as being entirely distinct, self-existent entities; but we will be foolish if we simply dismiss and 'demythologize' them as if they were merely outdated dramatic trappings which no longer mean anything in a 'scientific' age. The Gospel understanding of the demonic is more subtle and profound than the usual alternatives of credulity or scepticism allow. The New Testament uses the same terms 'principalities and powers', 'rulers' and 'authorities' to mean *both* supernatural forces *and* the very real powers – armies, nations, institutions or individuals – which represent them on earth. From the biblical point of view they are the same reality, seen in their spiritual or earthly aspects. In the book of Revelation each nation and each church has an 'angelic' counterpart in the heavenly sphere, whose wars and battles and turmoils reflect what is happening to them on earth. St Paul, when speaking of 'principalities and powers' means simultaneously both the visible, worldly authorities of government and law and the invisible, spiritual forces that stand behind them. These powers, whether viewed in either sense, are not inherently bad. On the contrary, they are created by God, and exist under his authority, and therefore should normally be obeyed.[9] Yet they remain fallen powers, and at any time may directly oppose God's will and become demonic in the fully negative sense.[10] Even so, the powers remain God's creatures and, like all creation, may ultimately be redeemed.[11]

In the Gospels the usurping demonic power is seen not only in sickness and sin but also in the warped application of the Law and the 'purity' system of social and religious domination as administered by the Scribes and Pharisees. The freedom Jesus brings is freedom from both personal and systemic evil; his confrontation with the demons parallels and symbolizes his confrontation with the Jewish authorities, and so is inseparable from it. Claiming God's own sanction, they cannot see that their own structures of domination have become demonic; and their fury mounts as Jesus' manifestly superior authority is vindicated by each miracle of healing, liberation and inclusion, until their hatred reaches the nadir of evil in accomplishing Jesus' death.

The Jewish authorities themselves, of course, held their power only by sufferance of the larger 'domination system' of the Roman Empire; and one or two miracle stories also hint at the equivalence between the Roman and the demonic powers. In the story of the healing of the centurion's servant, the reason given for the centurion's surprising faith is that he perceives in Jesus an authority comparable to but infinitely greater than his own. In the story of the healing of the Gerasene demoniac, it can hardly be coincidental that the demons are named 'Legion', and that Gerasa was the site of a brutal massacre of 1000 rebels by Vespasian's army. Here, at one level of meaning at least, the exorcism clearly symbolizes liberation from the domination of oppressive political power as well as from the supernatural power that was believed to lie behind it.

These observations are important because however we choose to understand the 'demonic' today, the Gospels mean us to grasp that the healing Jesus brings is as necessary for systems and societies as it is to individuals. We have seen that the healing miracles of Jesus must be understood as representative as well as individual healings, often implying the re-inclusion of a whole class of excluded persons. In the same way, the power of sin and rebellion against God, and the healing that they require, must be understood as operating corporately as well as individually. Every organization or community as well as every individual has its corporate 'demon' – that is, its spiritual as well as worldly aspect; and its potential for generating good or evil will depend on whether it is ordered according to God's will or against it. All systems and societies are therefore capable of becoming demonic in the worst sense. The past century has seen plenty of political systems whose demonic nature can hardly be gainsaid. The phenomenon of Nazism positively demands the vocabulary of the demonic, as a transcendent spiritual sickness which corporately possessed a people, and we have seen other extreme manifestations of corporate evil in more recent years, in Rwanda and elsewhere. We may be slower to recognize that family and religious systems too – including the most seriously and committedly religious, such as Pharisaic Judaism – are equally corruptible, equally capable of turning God's will upside down, his truth into hypocrisy, and his generous love and freedom into death-dealing forms of oppression.

Miracles and Faith

The Gospels' teaching about the purpose of miracles is paradoxical, at least at first sight. At first sight, the miracles seem to be intended as straightforward demonstrations of Jesus' divine power and evidence of the inbreaking of God's kingdom. Jesus says, in answer to the Pharisees who charge him with exorcising demons with the power of Beelzebub, 'If it is by the finger of God that I cast out demons, then the kingdom of God has come upon you'.[12] Jesus condemns the cities of Galilee and even his own disciples for their lack of response and 'hardness of heart' in face of the miracles.[13] When John the Baptist requires proof of his identity as Messiah, Jesus offers the miracles as evidence, pointing out how they fulfil the predictions of Isaiah about him.[14] In John's Gospel especially, the miracles (John always calls them 'signs') are said to be the very reason why the disciples believed in him in the first place.[15]

On the other hand, all the Gospels contain strong warnings about the dangers of being impressed by signs and miracles. Frequently, in Mark's Gospel especially, those who receive healing or witness a miracle are ordered to keep quiet about it. In Matthew's and Luke's list of Jesus' temptations in the desert (Matthew 4:1–11; Luke 4:1–13), two of the temptations involve the miraculous use of his own undoubted power: to change stones to bread, and to cast himself down from a height without harm. In John's Gospel, Jesus' own brothers want him to display his powers more widely in Judaea, but Jesus refuses.[16] When the Pharisees ask Jesus for a sign, the request is refused, with the comment that 'it is an evil and adulterous generation that asks for a sign'.[17] The only 'sign' to be given them is the sign of Jonah. Jesus offers them not a new miracle, but only the example of Jonah's submersion and rescue in the Old Testament, which is clearly meant to be understood as a symbolic prefiguring of his own death and resurrection.

How do we account for this ambivalence about the value of miracles? There can be little doubt that Jesus himself did perform miracles, but all the evidence suggests that he was extremely wary of being known simply as a wonder-worker. His commands to those whom he healed to keep silent and his depreciative remarks about 'signs' are at least partially understandable in the light of this reticence. There was certainly nothing unique about wonder-working. Although the reported nature and number of Jesus' miracles are striking, healers, exorcists and miracle workers were well known both in contemporary Judaism and in the Hellenistic world, and several of Jesus' miracles can be strikingly paralleled in the records of contemporary rabbis.[18] In the Gospels' estimation, miracles do not automatically indicate the high spiritual value of the one who works them. Even the 'sons of the Pharisees' perform miracles,[19] and the disciples themselves are given a share in Jesus' power to heal and exorcise, despite being as yet ignorant and unworthy, and in a real sense 'on Satan's side'.[20] So miraculous powers are certainly not of themselves any proof of great godliness.

As the story of his temptation suggests, Jesus' refusal to use his powers to further his own ends is presented in the Gospels as part of his own humility – the self-emptying of his divine power which culminates in his passion and death. The paradox of the partly veiled miracles corresponds to the paradox of the suffering, dying Messiah. Those around Jesus must understand not only his identity as Messiah, but also the true nature of his messiahship. Their commitment to him must not come from the attraction of power – or if it does at first, it must soon change to a deeper commitment, which will ultimately be prepared to follow in the same way of sacrifice, to take up the same cross and follow him. A personal belief in Jesus that goes deeper than self-interest and the mere worship of power is at least part of what the Gospels mean by 'faith'. It is for lack of this faith, or of the potential for it, that Jesus refuses to do miracles in his own home town, or for Herod. However, it is the evidence of such faith – or of the potential for it – even in the most unlikely characters (the centurion, the haemorrhaging woman, the Syrophoenician or Canaanite woman, the Samaritan leper) that seems to compel Jesus to perform a miracle even when his instincts as a loyal Jew make him initially reluctant. Faith, understood as openness to a relationship to God in Christ, is what makes the miracle 'safe' for the recipient, and not an idolatrous 'wonder', grasped at for its own sake.

It is often said that the theology of miracles is different in

John's Gospel, where they are less reluctantly performed and more obviously presented as a spur to faith and discipleship, but the difference is one of degree rather than substance. In John, too, Jesus is scathing about those who seek signs and wonders for their own sake,[21] but his estimate of their value is more nuanced. John's Jesus is prepared to tolerate, as it were, a lower stage of belief on the basis of his works, at least as a preliminary to a deeper faith in him. So in John Jesus tells the Jews, 'If I am not doing the works of my Father, then do not believe me; but if I do them, even if you do not believe in me, believe in the works, so that you may know and understand that I am in the Father and the Father in me'.[22] In a similar way he says to Philip, 'Believe me that I am in the Father and the Father in me; or else believe me for the sake of the works themselves'.[23] Three of the seven miracles in John's Gospel are directly paralleled in the Synoptics, and the other four are not dissimilar in content and theme and arguably also derive from Synoptic material. The fact that John prefers to call them 'signs' or 'works' rather than 'miracles' or 'acts of power' (*dynameis*, the usual Synoptic term) may relate to the greater element of symbolism in the Johannine miracles, where the actions of Jesus are made the focus of profound theological meditation on his identity and meaning. In the Synoptics the miracles are generally more 'eschatological' in flavour – that is, they express the inbreaking power of Jesus that was expected at the end time, driving back the dark forces that beset the world. But here too the difference can be overstated. As we have begun to see, there is a large element of theological symbolism in most of the Synoptic miracles too.

Eyes to See and Ears to Hear

The question of faith in relation to the miracles is closely connected to a particular theology of revelation that is also shared by John and the Synoptic evangelists. The faith that is a prerequisite of understanding the miracles, or which ideally the miracles should elicit, is a gift of God alone – a gift that God himself might choose to withhold. Mark's Gospel in particular explains Jesus' reticence about the miracles and the disciples' repeated failure to understand them with reference to a belief that God himself had willed a temporary spiritual deafness and blindness to come upon his people which actually prevented them from understanding. This paradoxical idea dated back at least eight centuries to First Isaiah who, burning with God's message, yet bitterly aware that the people seemed incapable of hearing it, envisioned God telling him,

> Go and say to this people 'Hear and hear, but do not understand!
> See and see but never perceive!
> Make the heart of this people fat, and their ears heavy, and shut their eyes;
> Lest they see with their eyes and hear with their ears and understand with their hearts,
> And turn and be healed.'
> And I said, 'How long, O Lord?'

Isaiah 6:9,10

This theology of God's deliberate self-concealment, and not least this particular text of Scripture, was important to all the evangelists and also to Paul as a means of explaining why it was that Jesus, the long-expected Messiah of the

Jews, went unrecognized and was finally rejected by his own people. It is no accident in Mark's Gospel that after the disciples had seen the two stupendous miracles of Jesus feeding the five thousand and then the four thousand, and still failed to understand, Jesus rails at them in Isaiah's words, 'Having eyes can you not see? Having ears can you not hear? And are your hearts hardened?'[24] Here the Twelve seem to incarnate, as it were, both the particular spiritual blindness of Israel and the general spiritual blindness of all humanity. The deliberately enigmatic teaching of the parables is also explained by reference to the same text of Isaiah.[25] In understanding both the miracles and the parables, only those who have an ear to hear can hear – and it is only God who can supply it.

Paul also quotes Isaiah 6:9 to explain the rejection of Christ by his own Jewish people, and speaks of what he calls 'a temporary hardening of their heart' willed by God. In his view, this 'hardening' by God has a definite and merciful purpose – to allow time for the gospel to be preached to the Gentiles.[26] This rationalization by reference to the Gentile mission is less evident in Mark and the other evangelists, but they all share the same view that for his own larger purpose God wills some to be blind to his message, and some to see. At the same time the hope remains that one day all the blind eyes will be opened and the deaf ears unstopped. Later on in his prophecy Isaiah himself had promised this time of ultimate spiritual healing, when 'the eyes of the blind shall be opened and the ears of the deaf unstopped',[27] and this text too has played an important part in the composition of the miracle stories. It is the basis of Mark's story of the healing of the deaf mute (the 'Ephphatha' miracle), where his use of an extremely rare Greek word meaning 'with a speech impediment' proves that he had the Greek text of Isaiah 35:5 consciously in mind, and intended the miracle to show its fulfilment.

All the Gospel miracles of Jesus healing the blind and deaf are to be interpreted in terms of this theology of revelation: their point is not medical but spiritual and theological. Whatever history may lie behind the stories of individual healings, their meaning and importance in the evangelists' mind is a universal, symbolic one: these miracles are about the potential of us all to be healed of our age-old, inherited spiritual deafness and blindness. One especially interesting example that demonstrates the case is Mark's miracle of the blind man of Bethsaida. In the dramatic plan of Mark's Gospel, Jesus spends the first half of it attempting to get the disciples to grasp his identity as Messiah, and the second half attempting to explain to them that his messiahship was not going to be of the kind they had expected. At the halfway point of the Gospel, at Caesarea Philippi, Peter gets the first half of the revelation right, and proclaims 'You are the Messiah' (Mark 8:29); but almost in the next breath gets it wrong again by refusing to accept that Jesus must suffer and die. Peter is half way to seeing; and it is no accident that immediately before this episode the miracle at Bethsaida precisely shows us a man who passes from blindness to sight in two stages. At first he sees 'people walking like trees'; then, at a second attempt, Jesus brings him to see plainly. So the pattern of the miracle story is itself a reflection of the pattern of revelation to the disciples. It is a further reminder, if one were needed, of the subtlety with which the miracle stories are woven together into the Gospels' literary structure and theological purpose.

The Inside Meaning Relates to Me

The main body of this book analyses almost all the Gospel miracles along the lines of the examples already touched on. It investigates their scriptural roots and literary origins, their theological purpose, their religious and social context, and the various levels of meaning they convey. I hope enough has been said already to show why this kind of analysis is essential, and how enlightening it can be. The analysis may seem academic, but learning to 'read the language' of the miracles in this way is far more than a merely intellectual exercise, and here too I hope enough has been said to suggest why. For us, who live at such a distance from the context in which the miracles were written down, and who are in general so ignorant both of the content and the character of Scripture, the background knowledge is indispensable if we are to get to the spiritual meaning. This is why I have seriously suggested that there is relatively little benefit in reading these stories at face value, whether in churches, schools, Bible studies or alone, without the guidance of a good commentary or an informed teacher. Indeed, it is often counter-productive to faith. (I can testify that the combined effect of Mr Davies and Miss Tomkins helped to put me off Christianity and the Bible for some years.) As Augustine says, it is all too possible for us to remain 'on the outside' of these stories, possibly marvelling at their element of wonder, or more likely dismissing them as obviously unbelievable. In either case we fail to be spiritually helped or nourished by them because we miss their inner meaning, and it is only their inner meaning, not the external wonder, that relates to our own real life and experience.

If Jesus once healed a haemorrhaging woman, so what?

It is a wonderful thought and a moving story, but with no possible bearing on me when taken at face value. But if I understand by this story that Jesus intended to overturn the taboos that labelled all women as unclean and helped keep them in subjugation, that may be of enormous significance for my own attitude, as a Christian man, towards women. Or if I am a woman who has experienced rejection or belittling by the Church, grasping the point of this story may produce a truly miraculous change in my own self-understanding as a Christian and a child of God.

If Jesus once turned 120 gallons of water into wine at a country wedding, so what? How does it change me? Or if he once fed five thousand people with a few loaves of bread, what difference does it make to me? But if I realize that these miracles point to a feast with Jesus that I can share in now, to a way in which I can be united with him now through receiving him sacramentally in bread and wine, then the miracle ceases to be a remote event of the past, and becomes part of a personal, present, joyful experience of Christ's never-failing gift of himself to his Church.

If Jesus once opened the eyes of a blind man, unstopped the ears of the deaf, loosened the tongue of a stammerer, so what? How can that help me? But if I find that his Spirit is still present and powerful to break down my own blinkered selfishness and make me see deep truths about God, myself and the world; or if he can overcome my stupid prejudices and fears and challenge me to change my self-protecting, hardened heart and open up in love to him and others; or if he can overcome my crippling self-enclosure and inability to relate to others, thus enabling me to speak out the truth he has shown me, then I too have been miraculously healed, and know what it means to be restored to the fullness of life.

All the miracle stories contain profound teaching which is of indispensable relevance to Christians and the Church today, teaching that all too often gets passed over because we do not get past the 'miraculous' packaging and the endless issue of 'did it happen?' I hope this book will help you take a fresh look at the miracles, to move closer to the 'inside' of them and to discover more of their relevance to you and your faith. You may even discover that miracles happen to you. In John's Gospel Jesus promises his disciples that they will 'do even greater works' once he has returned to the Father.[28] That may not mean that we discover in ourselves the gift of explicitly 'supernatural' powers – though they were not unknown in the early Church, and are not unknown in the Church today. In any case, as we have seen, Scripture itself does not set an especially high value on that kind of wonder-working. What matters more is that we come to share the same perception of the truth that impelled the evangelists to write the miracle stories in the first place. It is then that we get 'inside' the miracle, the miracle gets 'inside' us, and our eyes are opened.

Where the same miracle story is found in more than one Gospel, I have supplied the text of one version and refer to differences in the other versions, if they are relevant, in the commentary. Where certain miracle stories are different but close in theme – for example, the miracles of Jesus healing the blind, or the sea-miracles – I have put all the texts together and dealt with them in the same section. After the commentary on the miracles I have added a personal understanding of their meaning for today, followed by a selection of texts for prayer and meditation which I have found relevant and enlightening. I hope they will assist your own thinking and praying about the meaning in the miracles for you.

2

The Healing of a Leper

A leper came to Jesus begging him, and kneeling he said
to him, 'If you choose, you can make me clean'. Moved
with anger, Jesus stretched out his hand and touched him
and said to him, 'I do choose. Be made clean!' Immediately the leprosy left him, and he was made clean. After
sternly warning him he went away at once, saying to
him, 'See that you say nothing to anyone; but go, show
yourself to the priest, and offer for your cleansing what
Moses commanded, as a testimony to them'. But he went
out and began to proclaim it freely, and to spread the
word, so that Jesus could no longer go into a town
openly, but stayed out in the country; and people came
to him from every quarter.

Mark 1:40–45 (Matthew 8:2–4; Luke 5:12–15)

Commentary

The word 'leprosy' is used in Scripture to cover a number of
different skin diseases, and does not necessarily refer to the
particularly dreadful, wasting muscular and skin disease
for which the word is used today. Even so, the leper was an
object of horror in Jesus' society, not only because of the
terror of the disease itself, but also because it rendered the

sufferer ritually unclean – non-kosher. A leper was to be excluded both from corporate worship and from all social interaction, since not only was the disease regarded as physically contagious, but the ritual uncleanness it caused was also regarded as contaminating. Anyone the leper touched would have been similarly excluded from public worship and from all social intercourse until examined and declared clean again by the priest. Exhaustive rules concerning the quarantining of lepers are laid down in Leviticus, one of which was that if anyone approached, they were to shout 'Unclean! Unclean!'[1] Taking the viewpoint of a medical anthropologist, one commentator observes that both the sickness and the healing must be construed as much socially as individually:

> The sickness described in the Old Testament as leprosy may simply not be leprosy at all from a biomedical perspective. But from the sociocultural perspective – which is what the Bible always reports – this condition threatens communal integrity and wholeness and must be removed from the community . . . Jesus' activity is best described ethically as healing, not curing. He provides a social meaning for the life problems resulting from the sickness.[2]

The leper in the story breaks the levitical rules by apparently approaching Jesus without warning. It was shocking behaviour, which expresses both the man's desperation about his plight and the strength of his faith. This faith, and his instinctive recognition of Jesus' authority, are underlined by the fact that he kneels before Jesus (the word implies worship) and by the humility and the directness of his declaration, 'If you choose, you can make me clean'.

Jesus for his part breaks the rules in an even more shocking way by *touching* the leper. It was an unthinkable thing to do because, even if it was not a direct violation of the Law, it should have rendered him ritually unclean. The implication is, of course, that Jesus is inviolable. Instead of contamination flowing from the leper to Jesus, healing power flows from Jesus to the leper. The situation is similar in the healing of haemorrhaging woman, where instead of her contaminating Jesus, he senses the power passing from him to the woman. It is as if God's power is embodied in Jesus, and can pass from him to the bodies of others too.

Jesus' emotional reaction to the leper is extraordinary – more so than it appears in most English translations, which are too feeble. In the first place, we are told Jesus was moved with *anger*. Some translations, including the NRSV, substitute *moved with pity*, which is what we expect, but *anger* is the reliable reading. Then in the following verse, following the healing, where we are told '*he sternly charged the man and sent him away*', a truer translation would be, '*he snorted in fury and flung him out*'. The first word in Greek usually describes the flaring nostrils of an animal, and in the Greek version of the Old Testament it is the word used to translate Yahweh's *furious indignation* at his enemies. Jesus' fury is not to be understood as directed at the leper; it is the wrath of God himself faced with the power of evil that has held this man prisoner so long. It is worth noting that rabbinic tradition considered the leper a 'living corpse', and equated the difficulty of curing leprosy with that of raising the dead – a power that belonged to God alone.

From a Gospel point of view all sickness and disorder, as well as natural forces such as a storm, was as much evidence of demonic power as explicit possession. The language is therefore similar to that of an exorcism: Jesus is driving out a 'spirit of leprosy'. But just as the sickness has to be construed socially as well as individually, so must the exorcism. By challenging the laws pertaining to leprosy, and by generally overstepping the boundaries that demarcated the 'included' and the 'excluded', Jesus was challenging both the social system that maintained them and the 'Powers' that stood behind them. This is why the scribes and the Pharisees perceived Jesus' healings as such a threat. The exorcism of the 'spirit of leprosy' is a symbol and prelude to the ultimate cleansing and overthrow of their own system of control, and ultimately of all the 'principalities and powers'. Nevertheless, Jesus tells the man to show himself to the priests in obedience to the Law of Moses as laid down in Leviticus. This specified special sacrifices and ritual washings that had to be accomplished once a priest had verified the cure. He could then be welcomed back into society and corporate worship. The words imply Jesus' continuing care for the man, but they also demonstrate Jesus' own obedience to the law during his lifetime. This may be the meaning of the words *as a testimony to them* – as well as testifying to Jesus' power to heal, the man's compliance will show the priests that Jesus is not a lawbreaker. In the stories that follow Jesus will be accused of breaking a number of religious rules. Mark wants to show, as far as possible, that despite his struggle with the religious authorities Jesus was in fact observant of the law and taught others to obey it too.

Meaning for Today

To be a leper remains the proverbial expression for being an outcast. Perhaps the greatest importance of this miracle for the modern reader is that it is the first time in the Gospel that Jesus shows his will to touch the untouchable and embrace the rejected in the new kingdom he proclaims. The healing of the leper is the paradigm case, the first in a long list of excluded or marginalized categories of people in Jesus' society, whom Jesus includes whether by healing or simply by the manner of his dealing with them: lepers; tax-collectors; women – including those tainted by adultery, prostitution or the menstrual taboo; Gentiles; Samaritans; the physically defective of all kinds – the paralysed, crippled, maimed, deaf, dumb, blind; children. These were not the kinds of people with whom a rabbi was expected to consort; many of them, like the leper, were literally untouchable.

As H. Montefiore puts it, with the leper

> we begin to catch a new note in the ministry of Jesus: his intense compassion for the outcast, the sufferer, who, by his sin, or by his suffering, which was too often regarded as the result of sin, had put himself outside respectable Jewish society, who found himself rejected and despised by man, and believed himself rejected and despised by God.[3]

This last point expresses perhaps the most revolutionary aspect of Jesus' message. While Jesus certainly sought to be faithful to the Law, he flatly overturned the popular deduction that was often made on the basis of the Law: that these categories of people were the ones whom God himself hated. His message is precisely the contrary: that if anything, they are the most loved – if only because in their realization of their need they were open to the love that was offered to them.

Christ's affirmation of God's love for the outcast is crucial, not least because we have come to understand that the result of systematic social or religious rejection is that it is readily internalized by the rejected. The despised and excluded rapidly come to despise and reject themselves, to believe in their own rejection, to live up – or down – to it, and so to despair. 'Social exclusion' is no less a fact in our own society than in Jesus'. It is not a simple division between rich and poor – nor was it then. The more fundamental division still seems to be between the self-respecting and the self-despising. Who are our rejects and marginalized today? The socially inadequate, the semi-educated, the illiterate, the innumerate, the inarticulate, the chronically sick, the resourceless disabled, the addicted, the alcoholic, the homeless, the refugee, the asylum seeker, the criminal, the sink-estate dweller . . . Are these the objects of the Church's special care, the ones who find in the Church the kind of affirming, embracing, healing love that Jesus, in the teeth of charges of blasphemy and revolution, so determinedly offered to his troop of misfits and outcasts? And what about the Church's own outcasts and misfits, the victims of the prejudices that the Church itself has generated, and continues unrepentantly to generate – lesbians, gays, the divorced, single parents, cohabiting couples, and even today, within the Church's own life, women in general? 'How tedious!' some readers will think at this point. How 'politically correct'! But if a determination to include the despised and disadvantaged is what it means to be 'politically correct', then to the fury of his devout and respectable contemporaries, and despite what it cost him in the end, Jesus was, to a revolutionary degree, 'politically correct' too.

For Prayer and Meditation

In contrast to the traditional view that uncleanness was contagious, Jesus regarded holiness/wholeness as contagious. The physician is not overcome by those who are ill, but rather overcomes their illness. Thus Jesus touches people who have leprosy, or who are unclean, or sick or women, without fear of contamination. Jesus is not rendered unclean by the contact; rather, those whom society regarded as defiled are made clean. Holiness, he saw, was not something to be protected; rather it was God's miraculous power of transformation. God's holiness cannot be soiled; rather, it is a cleansing and healing agent. It does not need to be shut up and quarantined in the temple; it is now, through Jesus' healings and fellowship with the despised and rejected, breaking out into the world to transform it.

Walter Wink[4]

Jesus seeks always to restore the social wholeness denied to the sick/impure by the symbolic order. That is why his healing of the sick/impure is virtually interchangeable with his social intercourse with them. To one 'leper' he offers a declaration of wholeness, to another simply the solidarity of table-fellowship. Both acts defy the symbolic order that segregates those lacking bodily integrity; both challenge the prevailing social boundaries and class barriers. This is why Jesus the healer was a threat to 'civic order'.

Ched Myers[5]

They drew a circle that shut me out –
Heretic, rebel, a thing to flout.
But love and I had the wit to win –
We drew a circle that took them in.

Edwin Markham[6]

God lays upon everyone that he longs to bring into bliss something that is no blame in his sight, but for which they are blamed and despised in the world – scorned, mocked and cast out. He does this to offset the harm they should otherwise have from the pomp and vainglory of this worldly life, and to make their road to him easier, and to bring them higher in his joy world without end.

Julian of Norwich[7]

The owner of the house said to his slave, 'Go out at once into the streets and lanes of the town, and bring in the poor, the crippled, the blind and the lame'. And the slave said, 'Sir, what you ordered has been done, and still there is room'. Then the master said to the slave, 'Go out into the roads and lanes, and compel people to come in, so that my house may be filled'.

Luke 14:21–23

3

The Healing of the Paralysed Man

When Jesus returned to Capernaum after some days, it was reported that he was at home. So many gathered around that there was no longer any room for them, not even in front of the door, and he was speaking the word to them. Then some people came, bringing to him a paralysed man, carried by four of them. And when they could not bring him to Jesus because of the crowd, they removed the roof above him; and after having dug through it, they let down the mat on which the paralytic lay. When Jesus saw their faith, he said to the paralytic, 'Son, your sins are forgiven'. Now some of the scribes were sitting there, questioning in their hearts, 'Why does this fellow speak in this way? It is blasphemy! Who can forgive sins but God alone?' At once Jesus perceived in his spirit that they were discussing these questions among themselves; and he said to them, 'Why do you raise such questions in your hearts? Which is easier, to say to the paralytic, "Your sins are forgiven", or to say "Stand up and take your mat and walk"? But so that you may know that the Son of Man has authority on earth to forgive sins' – he said to the paralytic – 'I say to you, stand up, take your mat, and go to your home'. And he stood up, and immediately took the mat and went out before all of them; so that they were all amazed and glorified God saying, 'We have never seen anything like this!'

Mark 2:1–12 (Matthew 9:2–8; Luke 5:18–26)

Commentary

Removing the roof of the house seems a very drastic expedient to get Jesus to heal the man, though it might not have been as extreme as it sounds. We have to assume that roof was a relatively repairable wattle-and-daub affair, with steps leading to it from outside. Both features were typical of a Palestinian house. Mark's Greek is odd at this point: he says literally 'they unroofed the roof and having dug it out let down the pallet on which the man lay'. One suggestion is that the action is meant to symbolize a burial. The words 'dug out' and 'let the man down on a pallet' exactly describe what happens at a Jewish burial; and when he springs up after his healing at the command of Jesus to rise, the word used is the same as to 'resurrect'. All the Gospel writers regularly employ the literary technique called *chiasmus*, which means the balancing of themes and motifs at each end of their work. So it may well be that Mark intends us to see in this story at the start of the Gospel a kind of prefiguring of the resurrection at the end.

The main point of the story is Jesus' claim to forgive sins, a claim that shocks the bystanders. It is a fundamental assumption in Judaism that God alone can forgive sins. People may forgive one another, naturally, on their own behalf; but no one can do so on God's behalf or with his authority. Even the Messiah has never been credited at any period of Judaism with the authority to forgive sins in that sense. The Scribes' 'questioning in their hearts' was therefore entirely to be expected. The authority being claimed

35

here is more than messianic; it is that of God himself. The divine power of Jesus is further emphasized by the fact that he seems to know what is in the Scribes' thoughts by supernatural means (compare John 2:25: 'he needed no one to tell him what was in a person'). The reality of the claim to forgive authoritatively could not be proved on its own, of course, since it is an inward, spiritual matter. Hence the importance of the miracle. Jesus' question, 'Is it easier to forgive or to say to the paralytic, get up?', is not meant to imply that forgiving sins is literally 'easier' than physical healing. It is more a question of visibility. The physical healing proves the truth of the claim to exercise forgiveness.

A word of explanation is needed about Jesus calling himself 'the Son of Man'. Many volumes have been written about the precise meaning of the term, but these points at least are worth knowing:

1. The basic meaning of the idiom 'son of man' in Hebrew and Aramaic is simply 'human being' – a bit like the English expression 'every mother's son'.
2. In the visions of the book of Daniel, and especially in chapter 7, the term 'Son of Man' – still meaning 'human being' – is used as a symbol for Israel, whereas the Gentile kingdoms are symbolized as various beasts. So in Daniel the Son of Man is almost a title, but still not a real figure: only an image, a corporate personification of the people of God.
3. In later apocalyptic writing Daniel's image of the Son of Man develops into an actual Redeemer-figure who is expected to come at the end of time to save his people. Ideas about this Son-of-Man Redeemer had already begun to be fused with ideas about the Messiah shortly before Jesus' time.

4. There is some evidence that in Aramaic the phrase 'son of man' could be used as a polite or roundabout way of referring to oneself (almost the equivalent of 'one' in English).

In the present passage all these possibilities enter into the meaning of the term. Certainly Mark identified Jesus with the Son of Man, the expected Redeemer-figure (3), but arguments continue to rage as to whether Jesus would have applied this title to himself. Jesus may well, of course, have used the phrase in the everyday sense of (4), but it may already have been seen as ambiguous. However, it is perhaps most important to remember senses (1) and (2), which are often forgotten. Even when he comes to be seen as an actual Redeemer-figure, the Son of Man still means 'the Human Being' – the one who uniquely displays humanity in its true and intended form. *Jesus is the one who shows us what humanity is meant to be like, when it is truly in the image of God, because its relationship with God is unbroken.* That means that all other, fallen human beings, by accepting the salvation he brings and becoming 'incorporate' in him, can potentially become as he is, standing in the same relationship to the Father, with the same power and the same spiritual authority.

It is interesting that this last point is deliberately brought out in Matthew's version of the healing of the paralytic.[1] Matthew ends the story with the comment that the crowds were filled with awe, *and they glorified God who had given such authority to human beings.* In Matthew's thinking the authority to forgive is not limited to Jesus as the unique Son of Man. In his view, Jesus specifically handed on the authority to pronounce God's forgiveness to his disciples. Jesus tells Peter in chapter 16, and all the apostles in chapter 18, *whatever you bind on earth will be bound in heaven, and whatever you loose on earth will be loosed in heaven* (16:19; 18:18). The term 'binding and loosing' was applied to the authority of the rabbis to decide what was lawful or unlawful, and also to exclude people from, or readmit them to, the synagogue. Matthew believed Jesus handed comparable authority to the apostles to admit or exclude people in the Church, with the promise that *God himself would uphold their decision.* This amounts to Jesus handing over to the apostles his own authority to forgive in God's name. The same thing happens in John's Gospel, when Jesus says to the apostles on Easter day, 'Whose sins you forgive, they are forgiven; whose sins you retain, they are retained.'[2] On the basis of these texts the Anglican, Roman and Eastern Orthodox Churches understand the same apostolic authority to be handed on to bishops and priests in the ordained ministry.

The story of the healing of the paralytic also raises an important issue about the connection between sickness and sin. The fact that Jesus heals and forgives simultaneously might suggest that the sickness was the result of a specific sin on the paralysed man's part, or that he was an especially sinful person. That was the view of one strand of Jewish thinking, deriving from the ancient belief that God 'punishes sin to the third and fourth generation'.[3] Another view, which appeared later in Jewish history, denied any direct causal connection between misfortune and personal sin. The argument within Judaism is represented in the book of Job, where the older view is taken by Job's 'comforters', convinced that he must somehow have brought his sufferings upon himself, while Job, insisting on his innocence, represents the later view. The later view also seems to have been the view of Jesus himself. In Luke

38

13:2–6 Jesus denies that two groups of victims in recent tragedies were any more sinful than anyone else had been. And in John 9:2–3, when he is asked about a man blind from birth, 'who sinned, this man or his parents, that he was born blind?' he answers, 'neither this man nor his parents sinned'. Human sickness is to be linked not so much with the personal sin of the sufferer as with human sinfulness in general. As we have seen, from the Gospel point of view all disorder – sickness, sin, demon-possession, even natural phenomena such as storms and death – derive from the separation between God and a world that has fallen under the sway of satanic powers. Conversely the various demonstrations in the Gospel of the power of Jesus over sickness, sin, disorder and death are all equivalent signs that he bears the authority of God to drive back the darkness, and reclaim the world and human beings for their creator.

Meaning for Today

It is the faith of the paralysed man and his friends that makes the forgiveness and the healing possible. If both sickness and sin are the result of human separation from God, it is faith that bridges the gap and enables God to restore the relationship. Faith is not yet union with God, or even vision. But it is an opening up, a willed act of trust and hope that lets God in through the closed barrier of self. It is significant that Mark's Gospel tells us that the only place Jesus was unable to work miracles was in his own home town, 'such was their lack of faith' (6:5). It is this element of faith in those he heals that distinguishes the work of Jesus from mere magic or wonder-working, and that makes the miracle relevant to all people, whether or not they suffer from the particular ailment in the story. In this story the paralysed man does not ask to be forgiven his sin. There is no explicit repentance. But his faith and his great determination to get near to Jesus are clear. This commitment of his will is enough to enable Jesus to declare forgiveness: reconciliation between the man and his God.

The role of the companions is striking. As the story stands, it seems that the faith concerned was entirely theirs, and not the sick man's at all. It is they who do the hard work of carrying the man, and then of 'digging through' to Jesus for his sake. What they do for their friend is a perfect image of Christian intercession. It is the vocation of all Christians to carry others to God in their prayer and lay them before him. It is hard work, which can often feel like trying to 'dig through the ceiling'. The people we pray for may have no faith at all, or even knowledge that they are being prayed for. But God, it seems, can use our act of will to work for others: our prayer may open a channel that lets his grace into this world to work for them in ways we ourselves may never see.

What are we to make of the hint in Mark, and the clear statement in Matthew's version of the story, that not only Jesus as 'the' Son of Man, but also other 'sons of men', other human beings, have authority to pronounce God's forgiveness? One might understand it in two ways, which are not mutually exclusive. First, it may imply that where we forgive one another, God himself will also forgive, and not continue to hold the sins that we have committed against us. Jesus was repeatedly clear that *unless* we forgive one another we shall not be forgiven by God either. We may reasonably hope that *when* we forgive one another we *shall* be forgiven by God too. The second interpretation has already been described: the belief of some Christians that the authority to pronounce absolution – that is, to declare God's forgiveness – is handed on in every generation to bishops and priests through ordination into the apostolic ministry. This authority to forgive is exercised in confession, the sacrament of reconciliation. It is likely that some form of this ministry was already being exercised in Matthew's and John's churches, probably on the model of the rabbi's authority to 'bind and loose'.

Many Christians are suspicious of sacramental confession, but it does carry a special healing power for those who still need to hear the kind of *objective and authoritative* declaration of God's forgiveness that Jesus makes in this story. The Gospel insight that physical sickness and spiritual disorder are bound up with each other remains as true as it ever was. We are psychosomatic creatures, and our state of mind and spirit affects our physical well-being often more than we know. Most GPs will testify that the majority of patients they see are not so much physically ill as loaded down with intolerable burdens of guilt, depression, anxiety, loneliness or self-hatred. A doctor once admitted to me how much he wished he could exercise a power of absolution in the surgery, and lamented the fact that the Church is so ineffective in deploying this desperately needed ministry for the common good. As in the story of the paralysed man, the declaration of forgiveness in confession may or may not be for some particularly dreadful sin. More important is the opportunity to open oneself up in faith, and to be reassured of God's acceptance of our whole person, despite the sin and mess. To find a safe space in which to be able to say once in a while 'This is the real me, warts and all' is itself an immensely beneficial thing. But then to be told, with absolute authority, that this real me really is forgiven, accepted, loved and wanted by

God himself – that is perhaps the most healing thing a human being can hear.

For Prayer and Meditation

The power of faith is enormous. It is so great that it saves not only the believer; thanks to one person's faith others are saved also. We are not told that the paralytic at Capernaum had faith. But the men who brought him to Jesus and let him down through the roof had it. This is made clear in the Gospel: 'When Jesus saw their faith, he said "Rise, take up your pallet and go home"'. The stretcher-bearers believed and the paralytic had the benefit of being healed because of it. Perhaps your own faith is feeble. Nevertheless, the Lord who is love will stoop down to you, provided only you are penitent.

Cyril of Jerusalem, Catechetical Lectures 5:8

In pondering the story of the forgiving and healing of the paralytic, you may want to experiment by identifying yourself with the paralyzed man. . . . Do feelings come up which move you to pray about your situation? Jesus looks down on the sick man and recognises unforgiven sin and guilt as a barrier, a burden, an inhibition. Does he see in you anything that hinders your relationship with God, and yourself, and others? He reaches out to the man's helplessness. Does Jesus see you as paralyzed in some aspect of your life – stuck, unable to get up and go forward? Do you believe Christ can give you what he offered to the paralytic? . . .

If the authority to forgive sins were strictly a personal prerogative of Jesus, inevitably expiring with his death, incidents such as this would inspire little more than wistful envy. Instead, Jesus' followers insisted that he communicated this same authority to them. . . . The pardon that Jesus bestowed on the paralytic was not a phenomenon peculiar to his own ministry, but the first signs in a new era of relationship between God and humanity. To the disciples Jesus conferred personally and concretely God's forgiveness upon every man, woman and child who has faith in the gospel.

Martin L. Smith SSJE[4]

Happy are they whose sin is forgiven,
Whose sin is blotted out;
Happy are they whom Yahweh accuses of no guilt,
whose spirit is incapable of deceit!

All the time I kept silent, my bones wasted away
With groaning, day in, day out;
Day and night your hand lay heavy upon me;
My heart grew parched as stubble in summer drought.

At last I confessed my sin to you,
No longer concealing my guilt.
I said, 'I will go to the Lord and confess my fault',
And you, Lord, forgave the wrong I did,
You pardoned my sin.

Psalm 32:1–5

Confession is good for the soul.

anonymous proverb

Our God and God of our fathers, let our prayer reach you. Do not turn away from our pleading. For we are not so arrogant and obstinate as to claim that we are indeed righteous people and have never sinned. But we know that both we and our fathers have sinned.

We have abused and betrayed. We are cruel.

We have destroyed and embittered other people's lives. We were false to ourselves.

We have gossiped about others and hated them.

We have insulted and jeered. We have killed. We have lied.

We have misled others and neglected them.

We were obstinate. We have perverted and quarrelled.

We have robbed and stolen.

We have transgressed through unkindness.

We have been both violent and weak.

We have practised extortion.

We have yielded to wrong desires, our zeal was misplaced.

We turn away from your commandments and good judgment but it does not help us. Your justice exists whatever happens to us, for you work for truth, but we bring about evil. What can we say before you – so distant is the place where you are found? And what can we tell you – your being is remote as the heavens? Yet you know everything, hidden and revealed. You know the mysteries of the universe and the intimate secrets of everyone alive. You probe our body's state. You see into the heart and mind. Nothing escapes you, nothing is hidden from your gaze. Our God and God of our fathers, have mercy on us and pardon all our sins; grant atonement for all our iniquities, forgiveness for all our transgressions.

Synagogue Prayer for the Day of Atonement

When I look back upon my life nigh spent,
Nigh spent, although the stream as yet flows on,
I more of follies than of sins repent,
Less for offence than love's shortcomings moan.
With self, O Father, leave me not alone –
Leave not with the beguiler the beguiled;
Besmirched and ragged, Lord, take back thine own:
A fool I bring thee to be made a child.

George MacDonald: 'Confession'[5]

Our Lord Jesus Christ, who hath left power to his
Church to absolve all sinners who truly repent and
believe in him, of his great mercy forgive thee thine
offences: And by his authority committed to me, I
absolve thee from all thy sins, In the Name of the Father,
and of the Son, and of the Holy Ghost. Amen.

Absolution, Traditional Rite

Go in peace; the Lord has put away all your sins. Please
pray for me, a sinner also.

Dismissal after Confession, Modern Rite

4

The Wedding at Cana in Galilee

On the third day there was a wedding in Cana of Galilee, and the mother of Jesus was there. Jesus and his disciples had also been invited to the wedding. When the wine gave out, the mother of Jesus said to him, 'They have no wine'. And Jesus said to her, 'Woman, what concern is that to you and me? My hour has not yet come'. His mother said to the servants, 'Do whatever he tells you'. Now standing there were six stone water jars for the Jewish rites of purification, each holding twenty or thirty gallons. Jesus said to them, 'Fill the jars with water'. And they filled them up to the brim. He said to them, 'Now draw some out, and take it to the chief steward'. So they took it. When the steward tasted the water that had become wine, and did not know where it came from (though the servants who had drawn the water knew), the steward called the bridegroom and said to him, 'Everyone serves the good wine first, and then the inferior wine after the guests have become drunk. But you have kept the good wine until now'. Jesus did this, the first of his signs, in Cana of Galilee, and revealed his glory; and his disciples believed in him.

John 1:1–11

Commentary

In the Old Testament and in later Jewish literature many passages symbolize the messianic days as a wedding feast. As the prophets frequently depict Israel's unfaithfulness to Yahweh as fornication or adultery, so they promise that in the last days he (or his Messiah) shall 'marry' Israel again in an unbroken and eternal covenant. So it is no accident that many stories in the Gospels are about weddings: the story of the wise and foolish virgins;[1] the story of the king who gives a wedding feast for his son and no one turns up;[2] the story of the wedding guest who turns up but is thrown out for not wearing the proper clothes;[3] the story of the master who returns from the wedding banquet to find his servants ready or not;[4] the story of the guests who choose the highest and lowest places at the wedding feast.[5] Elsewhere in the Johannine tradition, in the climax to the book of Revelation, heaven itself is described as the wedding feast of the Lamb, the ultimate union of Christ and his Church.[6] In all these cases the wedding is a parable or symbol of the kingdom of God. The story of the wedding of Cana, though it has the form of a miracle story, and though Jesus himself, at least at the level of logic, is not the bridegroom, has to be understood within the same symbolic tradition. As John declares, this is the first of Jesus' 'signs' by which he showed forth his glory. The chief focus and meaning of that sign, as in all John's miracles, is the disclosure of the identity of Jesus himself; but this story – perhaps more than any other – is also packed with many other subsidiary signs and allusions.

The statement that this wedding happens 'on the third day' may itself be a clue that the story has an eschatological rather than a factual setting. This is a story about the new covenant, the new union of God in Christ with his people, which will be inaugurated by the resurrection on the third day. It is also a story about Jesus superseding the old covenant with a new dispensation of the Spirit. The chief symbolic action of the story is the replacement of water with choice wine, better than the wine the guests had been drinking. In the Synoptic tradition, too, new wine stands for the new life of the kingdom compared with the old. Once, according to Mark's Gospel, Jesus and the disciples attended a wedding and the Pharisees condemned them for not fasting. Jesus replied, 'Can the wedding guests fast while the groom is still with them?' Then he said, 'no one puts new wine into old skins; otherwise the wine will burst the skins and the new wine is lost. New skins for new wine!'[7] – meaning that the old ways and strictures of the Pharisees could not compare with nor contain the new teaching he brought. In John's story it is significant that the water in the stone jars is stated to be for the Jewish rites of purification. Probably even the number of jars is significant. Numbers are frequently symbolic in rabbinic and in Gospel writing, especially in Johannine literature, and the number six in *gematria* (rabbinic numerology) standardly symbolized deficiency, that which falls short. Furthermore, like the skins bursting with new wine in the Markan story, the water pots are said to overflow with the superabundance of wine when the change is effected, producing an extraordinary amount of wine – 120 gallons – which has often shocked over-sensitive and over-literalistic commentators. But, as with the feeding of the five thousand, the superabundance is part of the symbolism. Prodigious quantities of wine are a regular feature of Old Testament prophetic and apocalyptic descriptions of the last days.[8] One Jewish apocalypse contemporary with John names 120 gallons as the amount that will be produced from one grape when the last days arrive![9] The point is that in the new dispensation joy will unconfined, because the Spirit will not be given by measure. And the new will not compare with the past – as the steward declares, unconsciously inaugurating the messianic days with the marvellously ironic punchline, 'You have kept the good wine until now.'

The implications of the miracle for Jesus' identity are not exhausted by these associations with the symbolism of the messianic banquet. At many points of his Gospel John applies to Jesus features of the Old Testament's description of Wisdom, the female figure who personifies God's attributes and actions, mediating between him and humankind, and who is sometimes identified also with God's spirit, word or law. To a large extent John's description of Jesus as the eternal Word is equivalent to this identification with Wisdom – but '*Logos*' is more conveniently in the masculine gender in Greek, while '*Sophia*' is feminine. In Proverbs 9:5 and elsewhere Wisdom is said to prepare a banquet, inviting people to eat of her bread and drink of her wine – in other words to accept her message, which is none other than that of God himself. In rabbinic and Hellenistic-Jewish literature, too, there are numerous passages in which God's Wisdom or Word is symbolized as bread or wine. This symbolism even more clearly underlies John's version of the miracle of the feeding of the five thousand and the discourse about the Bread of Life that follows it. For John, Jesus embodies God's own Wisdom and Word, which had formerly only been symbolized by bread and wine. But Jesus *is* himself the *true* bread, the *true* vine. To receive him is to be united with him, and thus with God himself.

This identification of Jesus as Word and Wisdom with

wine and bread naturally suggests a further allusion to the Eucharist, as the sacramental means by which the believer is united with him. In the discourse in John 6, Jesus not only identifies himself as the 'Bread of Life', but explicitly connects the symbol with the Eucharist, speaking directly of his disciples 'eating his flesh and drinking his blood'. In the Cana story the connection is only allusive, but given the parallelism between the two miracles, in particular the supernatural abundance of bread and wine, and the clear connections with the 'messianic banquet', it is hard to deny that a eucharistic reference is present at Cana too. Both miracles were interpreted in a eucharistic sense in Christian art and theological writing from the second century onwards.

Possibly, too, Jesus is being presented by this miracle as the fulfilment of more than just the Old Testament tradition. For a contemporary reader in the Hellenistic world the changing of water into wine would immediately have recalled the liturgies of Dionysius, the god of wine, some of whose shrines had the same miracle attributed to them. Probably, however, the comparison had already been made in Hellenistic Judaism. In one passage Philo, comparing the inspiration of the Torah to that supplied by the pagan mysteries, says that 'it is the Word of God which will truly bring forth wine instead of water, and give your souls to drink with a divine intoxication'.[10] The Cana story is making a very similar point, except that the Word has now also appeared in flesh.

Jesus' words to Mary at Cana frequently puzzle or even shock modern readers. Her solicitude about the lack of wine hardly seems to deserve what sounds like a verbal slap – 'Woman, your concern is not mine' – especially when it is followed by Mary's humble reply, 'Do whatever he tells you'. To address someone as 'Woman' is not as rude in Greek as it is in modern English, but the same cannot be said of the second part of the saying. The literal words are 'What is there to you and to me?' The only other time the same idiom is used in the New Testament is in Mark's story of the exorcism in the synagogue, when the demons reply to Jesus, 'What is there to you and to us?'[11] Although much ink has been wasted trying to show otherwise, the question inescapably implies a gulf between Jesus and Mary – at best a divergence, and at worst hostility. This should not be so surprising. Several other Gospel passages imply a lack of understanding, even opposition, between Jesus and his family. In Mark's Gospel we are told they wanted to take him home because they thought he was mad;[12] in Luke, when one person declares 'Blessed is the womb that bore you', Jesus snaps back, 'Blessed rather is the one who hears the word of God and keeps it!'[13] Jesus frequently makes the point that what matters are not unredeemed human or family ties of themselves, but first the restoration of human relationship with God.

Perhaps the best parallel to these words to Mary is Jesus' rebuke to Peter at Caesarea, Philippi: 'Get behind me Satan! For you think as humans think . . .' (Mark 8:33). The point is that until Jesus' work is complete all human beings – even his mother and his best friend – are in some sense 'on the wrong side'. That is why Jesus continues, 'My hour is not yet come'. In John the 'hour' of Jesus is the hour of the cross, when reconciliation between God and humanity is accomplished – and when human relationships are also restored and re-ordered in the light of the new dispensation. And John's Gospel shows us this happening. At 19:25–27, which 'balances' the Cana episode, Mary reappears with the beloved disciple at the foot of the cross, and is again addressed as 'Woman': 'Woman, here is your son'; and to the disciple, 'Here is your mother'. Like all the words from the cross, these are loaded with symbolic meaning for the Church. Just as Peter will later be re-established as 'Rock' of the Church, here Mary is re-established as mother – but now not only as mother of Jesus' physical body, but as mother of the beloved disciple, and by extension, mother of all Jesus' beloved disciples: mother of his risen body, the Church. The double address to Mary as 'Woman' at Cana and at the cross may also be related to the picture of the Woman in glory in Revelation 12:27. Here, in an extraordinary complex of scriptural allusions, the 'Woman who brings forth the saviour' is iconically represented as the New Israel, the New Eve who treads down the serpent of Genesis, and the Mother of all 'who keep the commandments of God and the testimony of Jesus'.

Meaning for Today

Some years ago I led a party of pilgrims to the Holy Land, and visited the place that is (wrongly) identified with the Cana at which the miracle supposedly took place. In the church at Cana we did what pilgrims regularly do: the married couples in the party gathered around the altar, joined hands and renewed their wedding vows, after which I repeated the marriage blessing over them. It was a moving occasion, very significant for all those who took part. But I did not realize how painful it would be for a considerable number of people in the party who were unable to join in: those who were bereaved of their partners, those who had never been partnered, those who were lonely in their single-ness, those whose partnerships are not officially sanctioned by the Church. After the service I was horrified to discover how many of the group had been in tears in the shadows at the back, while the married people – symbolically standing in the light around the altar – had been celebrating their joy. Perhaps we should not have done it, not only because it caused too much pain to exclude so many people, but also because the miracle of Cana has almost nothing to do with marriage in the normal sense anyway. It might have made more sense to celebrate the Eucharist there, since that would have been far truer to what Cana is really 'about'. The marriage that the story relates is the marriage between God and his people, Christ and the Church. All are invited to the Wedding Supper of the Lamb, and no one is excluded.

The wine of Cana is the joy of union with God in Christ. It should be – can be – more profound, more ecstatic than the experience of human love. No doubt the Prophets and evangelists made the comparison with marriage because real, committed, sexual love is the nearest most of us get to feeling the mystery of God's own kind of love – the sort that really would give itself up for love of another, that knows what it means to lose oneself to find one's true self in the beloved. Some of the early Church Fathers, embarrassingly some may think, compare Holy Communion to sex. But why not? Receiving the Eucharist is the physical expression of the mutual love and self-giving between Christ and his Church. It is the outward act that both expresses and sustains spiritual and personal union. One might add, if it is absent, or too infrequent, it usually means there is something wrong.

Losing yourself in love really is the best thing in the world – and out of it. It is what the doctrine of the Trinity is about; it is the nature of God himself; it is what we mean when we say we are made in his image; it is the secret of the universe.

To be a Christian is to know, however deep down, and however much we forget from day to day, that our relationship with Christ is everything. Perhaps too many Christians bang on too loudly about their 'personal relationship with Jesus', so that it sounds fake and superficial. But equally, perhaps, too many Christians keep too quiet about it. Because it is true that this is the heart of it – everything else is no more than commentary. And to work on that relationship – to give it 'quality time', to pay attention, to listen, to try to please the Beloved – is no less important than in a human marriage.

But Cana and Holy Communion are about celebrating a corporate as well as individual relationship. The underlying joy that should mark the individual Christian's awareness of union with Christ should also be a mark of the whole Church. The Cana story does not hesitate to compare the joy of this celebration with drunkenness; perhaps it is no accident that the same image is used – or the same suspicion aroused – when the disciples are filled with the Spirit at Pentecost.[14] In the Western Church we are not good at joy, except perhaps in parts where it has been influenced by the Pentecostal or charismatic movement. Not that joy necessarily has to be expressed in loud and visible joyfulness. My own most profoundly joyful experiences of Christian celebration have generally been at highly formalized liturgies; but they were ecstatic experiences nonetheless – literally experiences of *ek-stasis*, of standing outside oneself and losing oneself in the Other. But alas, this is not the normal experience of people in our churches, whether 'high' or 'low' – which is no doubt why they are often so empty.

What about Jesus' words to his mother at Cana? There is comfort to be drawn from the attitude of Christ in the

Gospels to his family, and not least from this sharp encounter. At a time when many Christians take an uncritical or even idolatrous view of the family and 'family values' it is good to be reminded that Jesus' view was, to say the least, ambiguous, and that he himself clearly had problems with his own kith and kin. His teaching that all human relationships and all human institutions need redeeming – including motherhood and apple pie – is important to keep in mind, especially when ours prove difficult. God comes first, and everything else needs ordering in the light of our relationship with him. That means that whatever goes wrong, even the worst things, in our human relationships can still be healed and put right. As Christians we have been born again as God's children, and having been born again, we also have to grow up again, however old we are, into the people he wants us to be. For most people part of that growth involves healing wounds that were inflicted on us by the experience of broken relationships and the failure of human love. The wounds are not cancelled, but they can be transfigured, as God's unbreakable love shapes us into the people he wants us to be – eternally.

We are not born again in isolation, but as part of a new family, the Church of God, and we have the love and support of this new family to help us on our way. That means not only the Christian friends we know and see, but also the whole family – the saints in earth and heaven. Countless generations of Christians have drawn strength from a sense of fellowship in prayer with all the saints – 'friends on earth and friends above' – and among them Mary holds a special place in Christian devotion. Catholic and Orthodox tradition – and in recent years many Protestant commentators too – have found a scriptural basis for that devotion both in Luke and in the passages of the Gospel and the Revelation of John discussed above. But devotion to Mary should not rest on unreal sentiment, as the harsh words at Cana show. The gospel means us to see that by Christ's cross *all* must be healed and redeemed, including his own mother before she too finds her true place as mother of his new Body, mother of all his beloved disciples in the Church.

For Prayer and Meditation

Let my Beloved come, and taste
His pleasant fruits at his own Feast.
I come, my Spouse, I come, he cries
With Love and Pleasure in his eyes.

. . .

Jesus, we will frequent thy Board,
And sing the Bounties of our Lord:
But the rich Food on which we live
Demands more praise than tongues can give.

Isaac Watts: *The Church, The Garden of Love*

We become one body, members of his flesh and blood. Let the initiated understand. In order that we may become so, not only in love but also in fact, we must, as it were, melt into his flesh. This happens when we receive the food which he has freely given us, desiring to show how much he loves us. This is why he mixed up his own nature with ours. He has, as it were, kneaded our bodies and his together, so that we might become one thing, a body joined to a head. This is what happens to those who love each other strongly . . . Christ has done this for us, to bring us into a deeper love, and to show his love for us. He has given to those who desire him not merely to see him, but to touch, bite, eat, embrace his flesh, and so satisfy all their love.

John Chrysostom[15]

All were amazed and perplexed, saying to one another, 'What does this mean?' But others sneered and said, 'They are filled with new wine'. But Peter, standing with the eleven, raised his voice and addressed them: 'Men of Judea, and all who live in Jerusalem, let this be known to you, and listen to what I say. Indeed, these are not drunk, as you suppose, for it is only nine o'clock in the morning. No, this is what was spoken through the prophet Joel:

In the last days it will be, God declares,
that I will pour out my Spirit upon all flesh . . .'

Acts 2:12–17

Soul of Christ, sanctify me,
Body of Christ, save me,
Blood of Christ, inebriate me,
Water from the side of Christ, wash me,
Passion of Christ, strengthen me,
O good Jesu, hear me,
Within thy wounds hide me,
From the malicious enemy defend me,
In the hour of my death call me
and bid me come to thee,
that with thy saints I may praise thee
for ever and ever.

anonymous, fourteenth century

At Cana the wine did not simply come: the water became it. That is the divine method. When Christ came he did not come in a new order of being: he came in flesh, as a man. It was this real and actual human nature that he made divine. We are to follow that divine method. We are to take the water of life as we find it, and convert it into wine. Our lives and circumstances may seem incapable of fulfilling a divine purpose; yet it is through these that the divine purpose is to be fulfilled. . . . The artist, whatever his dreams and ideals of beauty may be, does not quarrel with this world and wait for another. He sets to work with the lines and colours that he finds, and realises his ideal through them. The Christian is the true artist of life . . . It is not too much to say that the main business of the Christian life is to go through the world turning its water into wine.

Cosmo Gordon Lang[16]

Hail, holy Queen, Mother of mercy,
Hail, our life, our sweetness and our hope!
To thee do we cry, poor banished children of Eve,
To thee do we send up our sighs,
Mourning and weeping in this vale of tears.
Turn then, most gracious Advocate,
Thine eyes of mercy towards us,
And after this our exile show unto us
The blessed fruit of thy womb, Jesus.
O clement, O loving, O sweet Virgin Mary.

anonymous, eleventh century

Be thou then, O thou dear
Mother, my atmosphere;
My happier world, wherein
To wend and meet no sin;
Above me, round me lie
Fronting my froward eye
With sweet and scarless sky;
Stir in my ears, speak there
Of God's love, O live air,
Of patience, penance, prayer:
Worldmothering air, air wild,
Wound with thee, in thee isled,
Fold home, fast fold thy child.

*Gerard Manley Hopkins from 'Mary
Mother of Divine Grace, compared to the
Air we breathe'*[17]

5

The Feeding of the Five Thousand
and the Feeding of the
Four Thousand

The apostles gathered around Jesus and told him all that they had done and taught. He told them, 'Come away to a deserted place all by yourselves and rest awhile'. For many were coming and going, and they had no leisure even to eat. And they went away in the boat to a deserted place by themselves. Now many saw them going and recognised them, and they hurried there on foot from all the towns and arrived there ahead of them. As he went ashore, he saw a great crowd; and he had compassion on them, because they were like sheep without a shepherd; and he began to teach them many things. When it grew late, his disciples came to him and said, 'This is a deserted place, and the hour is now very late; send them away so that they may go into the surrounding country and villages and buy something for themselves to eat'. But he answered them, 'You give them something to eat'. They said to him, 'Are we to go and buy two hundred denarii worth of bread, and give it to them to eat?' And he said to them, 'How many loaves have you? Go and see'. When they had found out, they said, 'Five, and two fish'. Then he ordered them to get all the people to sit down in groups on the green grass. So they sat down in groups of hundreds and of fifties. Taking the five loaves and the two fish, he looked up to heaven, and blessed and broke the loaves, and gave them to the disciples to set before the people; and he divided the two fish among them all. And all ate and were filled; and they took up twelve baskets full of broken pieces and of the fish. Those who had eaten the loaves numbered five thousand men.

Mark 6:30–44 (Matthew 14:13–21; Luke 9:12–17)

In those days, when there was again a great crowd without anything to eat, he called his disciples and said to them, 'I have compassion for the crowd, because they have been with me now for three days and have nothing to eat. If I send them away hungry to their homes they will faint on the way – and some of them have come from a great distance'. His disciples replied, 'How can one feed these people with bread here in the desert?' He asked them, 'How many loaves do you have?' They said, 'Seven'. Then he ordered the crowd to sit down on the ground; and he took the seven loaves, and after giving thanks he broke them and gave them to his disciples to distribute; and they distributed them to the crowd. They had also a few small fish; and after blessing them, he ordered that these too should be distributed. They ate and were filled; and they took up the broken pieces left over, seven baskets full. Now there were about four thousand people.

Mark 8:1–9 (Matthew 15:32–38)

Commentary

I have already dealt with these miracles briefly in chapter 1. As we saw, their first and most obvious *theological* purpose is to show Jesus as the new Moses, repeating one of the greatest acts of the Exodus: when the Israelites were fed in superabundance with manna from heaven. The similarity to the Exodus story is unmistakeable in both the context and the content of the miracle: like Moses, Jesus crosses the water into the desert; like Moses, he sits them down in companies, appoints helpers to distribute the food, and feeds them with miraculous bread in such quantities that there are basketfuls left over. Less obviously, Jesus is also acting in the person of Elisha. Some of the details of the story are taken from 2 Kings 4:42–44, where Elisha orders a disciple to feed 100 men with twenty loaves of barley. The disciple demurs, 'How can I set this before so many?', but Elisha replies, 'Thus says the Lord, "They shall eat and have some left"'. Taking the two together, the story is telling us that in recapitulating Moses, Jesus fulfils the Law; and in recapitulating Elisha, he fulfils the Prophets. This double witness of the Law and the Prophets to the true Messiah is important in the Gospels: the same point is made by the story of the Transfiguration, where Moses and Elijah appear in person with Jesus on the mountain (Mark 9:4; Matthew 17:3; Luke 9:30). The reference to Jesus taking pity on the people because they were 'like sheep without a shepherd' (Mark 6:34) recalls the appointment of Joshua by Moses in Numbers, 'so that the assembly of the Lord may not be like a sheep without a shepherd'[1] – a text that Mark may well have seen as predictive of Jesus, since in Greek 'Joshua' and 'Jesus' are the same word. Jesus, however, not only 'fulfils' Moses and Elijah and Joshua but also supersedes them. No less than in the sea-miracles, to which the two feeding miracles in Mark are each closely tied, Jesus acts here in the power and person of God himself. In Ezekiel God says, 'I myself will search for my sheep and rescue them . . . I will feed them with good pasture . . .'[2] In Isaiah it is Yahweh who will prepare the feast for all peoples when death is swallowed up for ever.[3] Or one may also see Jesus here, as in the miracle of the wedding at Cana, in the role of the eternal Wisdom of God, offering herself to human beings to in an overflowing banquet of bread and wine.[4]

In Mark's and Matthew's Gospels the feeding of the five thousand is followed by an almost identical feeding miracle two chapters on, but with different sets of numbers, loaves and fishes. Mark (but not Matthew) deliberately draws our attention to these numbers, when he shows us Jesus questioning the disciples about them afterwards:

'When I broke the five loaves for the five thousand, how many baskets full of broken pieces did you collect?' They said to him, 'Twelve'. 'And the seven for the four thousand, how many baskets full of broken pieces did you collect?' And they said to him, 'Seven'. Then he said to them, 'Do you not yet understand?'[5]

Clearly the numbers are symbolic, intended to point us towards interpreting the first miracle as a feeding for Jews, and the second as a feeding for Gentiles. The number five may be regarded as a 'Jewish' number because of its relation to the Pentateuch, the five books of the Law; the number four may recall the four winds, the four corners of the earth or the four 'beasts' in Daniel (the latter stand for the four Gentile empires that had overrun Israel). The number twelve recalls the twelve tribes, while the number seven had Gentile connotations, seventy being the conventional number of the Gentile nations. Alternatively, seven may simply represent 'fullness' here, as it does in many scriptural texts. This interpretation in terms of Jew and Gentile is strengthened by the fact that the first miracle takes place in a Jewish area near the Sea of Galilee, the second in the Decapolis, a predominantly Gentile area; and two different Greek words for 'basket' used in the two miracles are also said to derive from the two different cultures. The two stories, then, must have been understood by Mark and Matthew as a sort of prefiguring of the two-stage preaching of the gospel: 'to the Jew first, then to the Greek' in Paul's phrase. Possibly the second miracle was omitted by Luke and John simply because, in the time and context of their writing, the mission to the Gentiles was an undisputed fact, and is expressed by them in many other, less allusive ways.

The primary symbolic meaning of the bread is the Word of God, the message of salvation, which was to include Gentiles as well as Jews. The rabbis had already interpreted the manna in the Exodus story as a symbol of God's word, which he sends down to 'feed' human beings. It was an interpretation that was already suggested by the account of the story in Deuteronomy, where Moses warns the people that God had fed them with manna in the desert 'in order to make you understand that one does not live by bread alone, but by every *word* that comes out of the mouth of God'.[6] In his Gospel, John follows the feeding of the five thousand with a long discourse of Jesus on himself as the Bread of Life, adapting this already standard Jewish interpretation of the manna as God's word to his own theology of Jesus as the *Logos* incarnate.

In the commentary on John's first miracle at Cana in

Galilee, the connection was made with the common Jewish (and Gospel) portrayal of the messianic age as a feast, often a wedding feast. This feast itself was sometimes understood as a 'recapitulation' of the feeding on manna in the desert: Hosea prophesies that God will lead his people back to the desert where once he had fed them;[7] and one rabbi wrote that as the first Redeemer (Moses) fed his people with bread in the desert, so would the last (the Messiah) eternally (*Qohelet Rabbah* 1:9). In the apocalyptic tradition, *1 Enoch* promises that the righteous 'shall eat and rest and rise with the Son of man for ever and ever'.[8] The miracle makes this expectation of the banquet of the last days come true literally in the time of Jesus, but also points forward to its ultimate, eternal fulfilment in the kingdom of heaven.

As we also saw in considering the wedding at Cana, this link with the messianic banquet creates a further, obvious link for the Christian with the Eucharist, both in the general theme and in the detail. The actions of Jesus over the bread as described by Mark are exactly those of Jesus that he reports at the institution of the Eucharist in 14:22. One commentator remarks that 'to the early Christians the whole story would have been strongly reminiscent of their eucharistic worship, at which they too sat in orderly fashion while deacons brought round to them loaves blessed and broken by the celebrant'.[9] Even the fact that Mark mentions the grass was green is probably significant, since he is not given to adding merely incidental detail. Possibly he is pointing out that the month was Abib, the month of green grass – the time of Passover. It is certainly significant that John sets his version of the miracle explicitly at Passover time; and in the discourse on himself as the Bread of Life which follows it, Jesus identifies the bread explicitly with his own flesh *and* blood – making the eucharistic interpretation inescapable.[10] This, and the fact that from at least the early second century bread and fish appear in Christian art as symbols of the Eucharist, suggest the miracle was understood in this sense probably from the first.

The fish may seem something of a puzzle, when one considers the extent to which the miracle has been written so as to show these symbolic and scriptural connections. The Old Testament and later Jewish texts that refer to the Exodus story and the messianic banquet mention bread and frequently wine, but nowhere mention fish, and there is no evidence that the Eucharist was ever celebrated with fish as well as bread. There is one possible scriptural association: in Numbers 11:22-44, where Moses questions God's promise to feed the people in these words:

'Are there enough flocks and herds to slaughter for them? Are there enough fish in the sea to catch for them?' The Lord said to Moses, 'Is the Lord's power limited? Now you shall see whether my word will come true for you or not'.

There may be further connections, too, with the early use of the fish acrostic to stand for 'Jesus Christ, Son of God, Saviour' in Greek; and with the tradition reported in Luke 24:42,43 and John 21:13 that after the resurrection Jesus ate fish with the disciples. Finally, however, there is the obvious point that several of the disciples were fishermen, and Jesus' ministry took place in an area where fish were a staple of life. In whatever kind of meal lies at the historical base of the miracle story, it is not unlikely that fish would have played a part.

Meaning for Today

In chapter 1 I wrote about two different 'explanations' of this miracle, which I was given at school by two very different teachers. One found little more to say than that the miracle was a demonstration of Jesus' divine power. The other approached the story in a rationalizing, reductionist way, and opined that 'what really happened' was that Jesus and the disciples had taken their own bread and fish, but seeing the need around them, had been gracious enough to share with others who had nothing. Still others, who had also brought provisions which they had been keeping to themselves, seeing this example of generosity, were also inspired to share what they had with those around them, and so the example of sharing spread through the crowd, and in the end enough and more was had by all.

Both these interpretations contain some truth. Mark certainly does see this miracle, and all the miracles, as evidence of Jesus' divine power and identity. He also certainly understands the feeding as a sign of the feast of the kingdom; and the kingdom should, no doubt, be characterized by caring and sharing. Yet both interpretations are far from the main thrust of the evangelist's intentions as we have just teased them out. The problem with the first approach is that it says so little, and can only ever say so little, about practically every miracle, because it generally rejects a priori any non-literalist interpretation as fantasy or eisegesis. This ignores the plain truth about the gospel as a symbolic and allusive genre – a recognition of which is demanded by Jesus' own criticism of the disciples' failure to understand in Mark 8:19–21 – and shuts down any real engagement with the text. On the other hand, the second reductionist interpretation of the miracle as a call to greater charity hardly sounds like good news. Indeed, to interpret the story as a demand for harder ethical striving is almost the opposite of what it clearly was to the Gospel writers: a tremendous demonstration of God's free, miraculously overflowing generosity to his people. In this case the liberal reaction against a purely 'supernatural' reading leads to an equal impoverishment of understanding. The problem with both these interpretations is that they fail to come to terms with the existential character of Gospel writing, and so remain too objective and retrospective, endlessly hung up on the historical question 'what really happened?' The real aim of all the miracle stories – if they are not to be seen as mere wonder-working – is to strengthen and illuminate *faith*: that is, a *relationship* between Christ and the hearer.

The interpretation of Jesus feeding the five thousand that comes closest to Christian experience is the one that seemed most obvious to St John and the early Church. As they saw, the meaning of the miracle as it can be experienced by the reader is very largely the meaning of the Eucharist. Arguably the best commentary on it is the one that Scripture itself supplies: the discourse of Jesus on the Bread of Life in John 6:25–58. The Eucharist gathers up all the strands of allusion that the miracle weaves together. It is the present self-manifestation and self-giving of the one to whom the Law and the Prophets bore witness. In it Jesus still takes, blesses, breaks and gives the bread for his people. It is the Christian Passover, celebrating and making present the redemption won for us in Christ, as the old Passover celebrated and made present the redemption wrought for Israel at the Exodus. As the Passover manna came to be understood by the Jews as a symbol of the Word of God in the Law, or as God's own Wisdom indwelling us, so in the Eucharist we receive Christ the eternal Word of God, both in Scripture and in the sacrament. Like the Passover, the Eucharist is the Church's family meal, which sustains us through the 'desert' of earthly life. It is for all people and races: 'the Jew and also the Greek'. It prefigures, but also actualizes, the 'banquet' of heaven, symbolizing the mystical union with God and one another which we will fully know there, but of which we also have a foretaste in Holy Communion. It is the same, continuing miracle, through which the life of God himself is still imparted to us, still superabundant and unfailing, in all times and in all places.

For Prayer and Meditation

I am the bread of life. Your ancestors ate the manna in the wilderness, and they died. This is the bread that comes down from heaven so that one may eat of it and not die. I am the living bread that came down from heaven. Whoever eats this bread will live for ever.

John 6:48-51

'I am the living bread which comes down from heaven'. It is 'living' because it was Jesus who came down from heaven. The manna also came down from heaven, but the manna was only a shadow, this is the reality. Those who heard were terrified at this. It was too much for them, they thought it was impossible. But believers know they are the body of Christ, provided they do not neglect to *be* the body of Christ. One must *be* the body of Christ, if one is to live by the Spirit of Christ. So whoever wants to live, must live as part of the body.

Augustine of Hippo, Homilies on the Gospel of John 26:13

When you eat this food and drink this wine, they will be transformed into your substance. Equally you will be transformed into the body of Christ, if you live in obedience and faithfulness. The Apostle reminds us of the prediction in scripture: 'Two will become one flesh'. And elsewhere in reference to the eucharist itself, he asserts, 'Because there is one bread, we who are many are one body'. You, therefore, begin to receive what you already begin to be.

Augustine of Hippo, Sermons 227

As this broken bread was scattered on the mountains and then, being gathered together, became one, so may thy Church be gathered together from the ends of the earth into thy kingdom.

Extract from the Eucharistic Prayer of the Didache (second century)

O sacred banquet, in which Christ is received,
The offering of his passion is renewed,
The mind is filled with grace,
And a promise of future glory given to us!

anonymous, traditional

Bread of heaven, on thee we feed,
for thy flesh is meat indeed;
ever may our souls be fed
with this true and living bread;
day by day with strength supplied
through the life of him who died.

Josiah Conder

6

Two Sea-Miracles

1. Jesus Calms the Storm

When evening had come, Jesus said to them, 'Let us go across to the other side'. And leaving the crowd behind, they took him with them in the boat, just as he was. Other boats were with him. A great windstorm arose, and the wind beat into the boat, so that the boat was already being swamped. But Jesus was in the stern, asleep on the cushion; and they woke him up and said to him, 'Teacher, do you not care that we are perishing?' He woke up and rebuked the wind, and said to the sea, 'Peace! Be still!' Then the wind ceased, and there was a great calm. He said to them, 'Why are you afraid? Have you still no faith?' And they were filled with great awe, and said to one another, 'Who then is this, that even the wind and the sea obey him?'

Mark 4:35–41 (Matthew 8:18–27; Luke 8:22–25)

2. Jesus Walks on the Water

When evening came, the boat was out on the sea, and Jesus was alone on the land. When he saw that they were

71

straining at the oars against an adverse wind, he came towards them early in the morning, walking on the sea. He intended to pass them by. But when they saw him walking on the sea, they thought it was a ghost, and cried out; for they all saw him and were terrified. But immediately he spoke to them and said, 'Take heart; it is I; do not be afraid'. Then he got into the boat with them and the wind ceased. And they were utterly astounded.

Mark 6:47–52 (Matthew 14:25–33; John 6:15–21)

Commentary

Within a long strand of Old Testament tradition, the sea was especially associated with evil powers. According to an ancient creation myth, which emerges in numerous texts, when he made the world and separated out the dry land, God had to combat monstrous forces of chaos that lived in, or were identified with, the waters of the sea. This primal battle was recalled in many verses of the Psalms and the Prophets, especially those dating from periods when Israel was passing through storms of war, invasion or persecution. Frequently the Psalmist or Prophet reminds God (and his readers) of what God has done in the past, and of the need for him to deploy the same power in the present:

> O Lord God of hosts, who is like you?
> Your power and your faithfulness are all about you.
> You rule the raging of the sea,
> when its waves surge you still them.
> You crushed Rahab like a carcass,
> you scattered your enemies by your mighty arm.

Psalm 89:8–10

Rahab was one of the names of the primal sea-monster, or perhaps a personification of the chaos itself, with which God had to do battle. In later Jewish religion the sea retained its evil associations as the natural abode of demons; rabbinic theology provided for both a 'fiery' and a 'watery' hell. (This is probably why, in the healing of the Gerasene demoniac, the demons end up there, in their proper place.) In the first of these two sea-miracles, when Jesus calms the storm he addresses it as if it were a quasi-personal force. He uses exactly the same word that he used to the demoniac in the synagogue[1] – a curious verb, which means literally 'Be muzzled!' – in the way one might subdue a rabid animal. There is some evidence to suggest that the word was already in liturgical use by exorcists to command the 'binding' of demons. In Mark's mind the calming of the storm shows Jesus' power over the forces of supernatural evil just as clearly as the explicit healing of the possessed. Both miracles show him driving back and 'binding' the demonic powers that have invaded the world – two skirmishes in the war which, in Mark's Gospel, begins with the temptation in the wilderness and ends with the triumph of the cross.

A number of other Old Testament passages that dwell on the theme of Yahweh's battle with the sea-monsters seem to have contributed particular details of the story. The best known is Psalm 107:23–29, which forms part of a litany of different ways and occasions in which God has shown his power to save his people in times of trouble. It is worth quoting in full:

Some went down to the sea in ships,
doing business on the mighty waters;
they saw the deeds of the Lord,
his wondrous works in the deep.

For he commanded and raised the stormy wind
which lifted up the waves of the sea.
They mounted up to heaven, they went down to the
depths;
their courage melted away in their calamity;
they reeled and staggered like drunkards,
and were at their wits' end.
Then they cried to the Lord in their trouble,
and he brought them out from their distress.
He made the storm be still,
and the waves of the sea were hushed.

This passage may well have given Mark's story its general
shape; and the fact that it refers to a number of ships may
well be the reason why Mark's story adds, without any
further explanation or follow-up, 'And a number of boats
were with him'.

While Jesus calmly sleeps the sailors panic and call to him
to wake: does he not care that they are in danger of drowning? This motif, too, probably derives from similar Old
Testament texts, where the author does not hesitate to call
on God to wake up and do something for his people in their
time of distress. One example seems particularly close to
Mark's story:

Awake, awake, put on strength,
O arm of the Lord!
Awake, as in days of old,
the generations of long ago!
Was it not you who cut Rahab in pieces,
who pierced the dragon?
Was it not you who dried up the sea,
the waters of the great deep;

who made the depths of the sea a way
for the redeemed to cross over?

Isaiah 51:9–10

Another similar text is Psalm 44:23:

Rouse yourself! Why do you sleep, O Lord?
Awake, do not cast us off forever!

The second miracle, in which Jesus walks on the water,
relates more specifically to a series of Old Testament texts
that refer specifically to Yahweh's power to walk *on* or
through the waves. Here the writers have in mind both the
creation myth of God's wrestling with the waters of chaos
and the Exodus story in which he went ahead of his people
to lead them through the sea into freedom:

Thus says the Lord,
who makes a way in the sea,
a path in the mighty waters . . .

Psalm 43:16

Yahweh alone stretched out the heavens
and trampled the waves of the sea,
made the Bear and Orion,
the Pleiades and the chambers of the south.

Job 9:8

Your way was through the sea,
your path through the mighty waters;
yet your footsteps were unseen.

Psalm 77:19

In both the sea-miracles it is important to grasp clearly what Mark is telling us. In all the Old Testament passages that underlie these stories, the point is being made that *God alone* rules the waves and walks through the waters; *God alone* defeated the primal sea-monster; and *God alone* can defeat the demonic powers of chaos and evil. When Mark gives us the chorus of the disciples at the end of the first miracle, '*Who is this that even the wind and the sea obey him?*', he is forcing us to draw the inevitable conclusion which the disciples, Mark tells us, were still too stupid, blind and faithless to draw for themselves. That conclusion is that in some undefined sense – but certainly in the most real and powerful sense – Jesus *is* Yahweh himself present on earth. Compared with the other Gospels, it is often said that Mark has a relatively 'low Christology' – meaning that, generally speaking, in Mark's Gospel Jesus is relatively more 'human' than in the other Gospels, his divinity is more subtly and reticently conveyed. Mark has no Prologue, as John has, to explain Jesus' eternal existence as the divine Word; no virginal conception, as Matthew and Luke have, to show that he was divine even from the womb. Nevertheless, here it is unmistakeably clear that for Mark also Jesus was no less than *Immanuel*, 'God among us'.

The same conviction is confirmed in the second miracle in an even subtler way. Mark notes that when walking on the water Jesus 'intended to pass them by', which seems to make little sense when we have already been told that he set out to walk towards them. It begins to make sense, however, in the light of a number of passages where God reveals himself in 'passing by' his people or his prophets, and especially in Exodus 33:18,19, where Yahweh 'passes by' Moses, and discloses to him his glory and his name:

Moses said, 'Show me your glory I pray'. And he said, 'I will make all my goodness pass by you, and I will proclaim before you my name, the Lord (YHWH)'.

The holy, unpronounceable name that is disclosed to Moses is Yahweh, I AM. And it is no accident that having 'passed by' them on the water, what Jesus says to the terrified disciples is not 'It is I', as our English Bibles misleadingly translate it, but literally in the Greek, 'Take heart: I AM (*ego eimi*); have no fear'. Here, no less than in John's Gospel – but much more hiddenly – Jesus is himself seen to be none other than Yahweh, the great I AM, the source and end of all that is.

Theologically, then, the purpose of these two miracles is clear. Like the Transfiguration, they are *theophanies*, manifestations of Jesus' divinity, his oneness with God himself. Within Mark's Gospel they form part of a dramatic pattern of progressive disclosure of Jesus' identity and destiny (counterbalanced with a pattern of misunderstanding, blindness and betrayal on the part of the disciples), which will culminate in the story of his passion and resurrection.

At the same time, like the Old Testament authors whose work has entered into his, Mark also has another purpose relating to his own community. In all probability Mark was writing for a church, possibly in Rome, that was facing political hostility and the threat or reality of persecution. In the face of danger they may well have felt buffeted, in danger of going under. They may well have been wondering why Christ was so slow to act – was he asleep? In these stories Mark is reminding them that, even if Christ might seem indifferent while the ark of his church was being rocked by persecution and suffering, they must have faith. As long as Jesus was with them, there was no need to fear that the powers of evil might prevail. If some were fearing that he was indeed asleep or, worse, had left them alone in the boat, there is particular poignancy in the culmination of the second miracle: ' "Take heart, I AM; do not be afraid". Then he got into the boat and the wind ceased.' As one commentator puts it:

> To the Roman Church, bereft of its leaders and confronted by a hostile government, it must indeed have appeared that *the wind was contrary and progress difficult and slow*: faint hearts may even have begun to wonder whether the Lord himself had not abandoned them to their fate, or to doubt the reality of Christ. They are to learn from this story that they are not forsaken, that the Lord watches over them unseen (as Jesus had done from the land – vs 47,48) – and that He Himself, no phantom but the Living One, Master of winds and waves – will surely come quickly for their salvation, even though it be *in the fourth watch of the night*.[2]

Matthew's version of the story of Jesus walking on the water is expanded with the story of Peter attempting to do the same:

> Peter answered him, 'Lord if it is you, command me to come to you on the water'. He said, 'Come'. So Peter got out of the boat, started walking on the water, and came towards Jesus. But when he noticed the strong wind he became frightened, and beginning to sink he cried out, 'Lord save me!' Jesus immediately reached out his hand and caught him, saying to him, 'You of little faith, why did you doubt?'[3]

Most commentators regard this as Matthew's own elaboration of Mark's story. Peter here is the representative disciple. He sets out in faith, in response to Jesus' call, and because all things are possible to one who has faith, at first he is able to do what his master does (as Jesus promises in Matthew 10:25; 17.20). But in the face of fear and danger his faith falters, until he calls on the Lord again to restore it. Here even more than in Mark's version of the story the emphasis is on holding firm to faith in time of trouble. It is a reassurance to the individual disciple, as well as to the Church as a whole, that Christ is always at hand, even when faith falls short.

Meaning for Today

Long before Mark wrote these miracle stories, for the authors of the Old Testament the storm was a symbol of all the tribulations and disasters that can befall the individual and the community. For the most part they themselves wrote at times of tribulation and disaster, both personal and communal. But through the storms they clung to the conviction that simply because God is God, he was able to bring them through. And through repeated experience of storm and disaster that conviction only strengthened and grew. The sea-miracles in the Gospels apply that same conviction to Jesus, focusing all the confidence that the Prophets and Psalmists professed in Yahweh on to a real, historical figure: Jesus Christ. Because we are so used to these stories, we risk missing how totally extraordinary this fact is: that writers who were Jews, trained in the law, raised in the most monotheistic of faiths, should believe that in Jesus Yahweh's own power and authority had literally walked this earth in a human being.

However used or unused we may be to the ways of the sea, the image of the storm has lost none of its power. These miracles have strengthened countless millions of Christians, whether going through the tempests of corporate persecution, like Mark's own Church, or through personal storms of illness, loss, betrayal, bereavement or breakdown. There can hardly be a Christian who cannot immediately identify with Peter, losing faith in face of fear and trouble, sinking in panic, then gathered up and rescued by forgiving love. However much modern Christians may wonder what did or didn't happen on the Sea of Galilee over 2000 years ago; however much we may struggle to understand what it means to say that Jesus was God on earth, as Mark and the early Church were so unshakeably clear he was – it remains a fact of Christian experience that these miracles 'work'. Their message is true. Not usually, perhaps, in the sense that physical storms are calmed, or that Christians walk on water. But certainly in the sense that Christ's words still have extraordinary power to bring 'a great calm' in times of turmoil and chaos – when we have faith, however faltering, that he is who he is: 'Peace, be still. Do not be afraid. I AM.'

For Meditation and Prayer

Be still, my soul:
your God will undertake
to guide the future
as he has the past.
Your hope, your confidence
let nothing shake,
all now mysterious
shall be clear at last.

Be still, my soul:
the tempests still obey
his voice, who ruled them
once on Galilee.

Katharina von Schlegel, trans. Jane L. Borthwick

'Be still and know that I am God.
I will be exalted among the nations,
I will be exalted on the earth'.
The Lord of hosts is with us;
the God of Jacob is our refuge.

Psalm 46:10–11

Save me O God,
for the waters have come up to my throat.
I sink in deep mire
where there is no foothold.
I have come into deep waters
and the flood sweeps over me.
I am wearied with my crying;
my throat is parched.
My eyes grow dim
with waiting for my God.

Psalm 69:1–3

Deep calls to deep in the roar of your waters;
all your waves and breakers have gone over me.

Psalm 42:7

That little ship offers us a figure of the Church, for she is
tossed by sea (that is, the world) and by the waves (that
is, persecutions and temptations), with the Lord patiently
sleeping, as it were, until awakened by the prayers of the
saints, he checks the world and restores tranquillity to his
own.

Tertullian[4]

Give us Lord the grace to walk by faith,
through every storm of life to keep our eyes on you.
And when we fail to see, or start to sink,
stretch out your hand to raise us up.
So may we learn to hold to you through good and ill,
until we come to the haven where we would be,
in everlasting joy and peace.

Jeffrey John

Blessed are all thy saints, O God and King, who have
travelled over the tempestuous sea of this mortal life, and
have made the harbour of peace and felicity. Watch over
us who are still in our dangerous voyage; and remember
those who lie exposed to the rough storms of trouble and
temptation. Frail is our vessel, and the ocean is wide; but
as in thy mercy thou hast set our course, so steer the
vessel of our life toward the everlasting shore of peace,
and bring us at last to the quiet haven of our heart's
desire, where thou, O God, art blessed, and livest and
reignest for ever and ever.

Augustine of Hippo

He lay with quiet heart in the stern asleep:
Waking, commanded both the winds and sea.
Christ, though this weary body slumber deep,
Grant that my heart may keep its watch with thee.
O Lamb of God that carried all our sin,
Guard thou my sleep against the enemy.

Alcuin of York

7

The Gerasene Demoniac

They came to the other side of the sea, to the country of the Gerasenes. And when Jesus had stepped out of the boat, immediately a man with an unclean spirit met him. He lived among the tombs, and no one could restrain him any more, even with a chain; for he had often been restrained with shackles and chains, but the chains he wrenched apart, and the shackles he broke in pieces; and no one had the strength to subdue him. Night and day among the tombs and on the mountains he was always howling and bruising himself with stones. When he saw Jesus from a distance, he ran and bowed down before him; and he shouted at the top of his voice, 'What have you to do with me, Jesus, Son of the Most High God? I adjure you by God, do not torment me'. For Jesus had said to him, 'Come out of the man, you unclean spirit!' Then Jesus asked him, 'What is your name?' He replied, 'My name is Legion, for we are many'. He begged him earnestly not to send them out of the country. Now there on the hillside a great herd of swine was feeding; and the unclean spirits begged him, 'Send us into the swine; let us enter them'. So he gave them permission. And the unclean spirits came out and entered the swine; and the herd, numbering about two thousand, rushed down the steep bank into the sea, and were drowned into the sea.

The swineherds ran off and told it in the city and in the country. Then people came to see what it was that had happened. They came to Jesus and saw the demoniac sitting there, clothed and in his right mind, the very man who had had the legion; and they were afraid. Those who had seen what had happened to the demoniac and to the swine reported it. Then they began to beg Jesus to leave their neighbourhood. As he was getting into the boat, the man who had been possessed by demons begged him that he might be with him. But Jesus refused, and said to him, 'Go home to your friends, and tell them how much the Lord has done for you, and what mercy he has shown you'. And he went away and began to proclaim in the Decapolis how much Jesus had done for him; and everyone was amazed.

Mark 5:1–20 (Matthew 8:28–34; Luke 8:26–39)

Commentary

The naming of this miracle poses a problem. Different manuscripts of the Gospels use different titles for the place where the miracle happened. Some say Gerasa, others Gadara, still others Gergesa. Gergesa is otherwise unknown and can be discounted. Both Gerasa and Gadara exist, and are in the territory of the Decapolis. Gerasa is further from the Sea of Galilee than Gadara, and so makes less sense in view of the story about the drowning pigs, but Gerasa is best attested in the manuscripts.

The best explanation for the confusion is that the story was originally associated with Gadara, but was located by Mark at Gerasa because the place had recently become notorious as a centre of Jewish revolt which was brutally put down by the Roman army. The historian Josephus reports that in 67AD Vespasian's general Lucius Annius slaughtered 1000 rebels who were besieged in Gerasa, then destroyed both it and the surrounding villages.[1] The fact that the demoniac is called by the Latin name 'Legion' strongly suggests that Mark saw a link between the exorcism of the evil powers occupying the demoniac and this extreme act of Roman oppression. This is further confirmed by the description of the pigs. Since 2000 pigs are specified, Mark may have confused the number of a Roman 'legion' (6000) with that of a battalion (which was 2000 – the probable number of Lucius's men). Several of the Greek words used here ('herd' of pigs; the pigs were 'commanded' and 'charged' into the sea) also point to the association between the expelled demonic powers and the military.

This should not surprise us. As noted in Chapter 1, New Testament theology makes a strong association between the 'powers that be' on the political stage, and the supernatural 'powers that be' who are believed to stand behind them. Just as there is a clear identification between the evil powers and the 'domination system' of the Scribes and Pharisees in the Gospels, an identification that becomes very clear in Jesus' quarrel with the Pharisees about exorcism, so there is also here a clear identification between the Roman power and the supernatural powers who control them. It has been observed that the oppression of one culture by another frequently becomes reflected or expressed through the phenomenon of possession. When this occurs, personal exorcism becomes symbolic of corporate liberation from oppression:

Miracle stories involving exorcism can be understood as symbolic action which breaks the demonic spell of all-pervading dependence ... The fact that the charismatic miracle workers of the first century AD were invariably from the east which was firmly under Roman domination invites the hypothesis that . . . the politically inferior proclaims and propagates his superiority on the level of miraculous activity.[2]

This exorcism then, proclaims (among other things, as we shall see) that even the power of Rome will ultimately be no match for the liberating power of God in Christ.

It is not an accident that this exorcism follows immediately after the story of Jesus calming the storm. As we saw, Jesus addressed the storm in the same language he had already used to exorcise a demon. Both the sea-miracles and the exorcisms perform the same function, to show Jesus as the agent of Yahweh's power over *all* the dark forces that hold this world in thrall. The very dramatic character of this particular story, the extreme nature of the case of possession and the very large number of demons only serve to underline the extent of that power. But as well as this link in terms of theological motive, there is also an underlying literary base that connects this miracle story with the calming of the storm. The two stories seem to have been put together deliberately to provide a kind of double fulfilment of Psalm 65:7:

> You silence the roaring of the seas,
> the roaring of the waves,
> and the madness of the nations [= Gentiles].

In this verse the Psalmist praises Yahweh's might, doubly displayed in his power to quell the sea and in his power to defeat the 'furious' Gentiles who were threatening Israel.

87

The whole of Psalm 65 probably caught Mark's attention because it so accurately reflected the ambiguities of his own position. The Psalmist deplores the raging madness of the Gentile powers who are warring against his own people, yet still looks forward to the day when even they will be stilled, and included within the blessings of Israel. The promise is universal: 'to you, Lord, all flesh shall come' . . . 'you are the hope of all the ends of the earth' (Psalm 65:2,5). Moreover, Mark, while deploring the current brutalities of Roman oppression in his own land, remains committed to the Gentile mission. For him, both Jew and Gentile need rescuing from the domination of hostile powers by the liberating power of Christ.

Two other Old Testament texts seem to have supplied some of the details of the story. First, Psalm 68:6 (in the Greek version, which Mark was using) runs:

God makes the solitary dwell in a home,
leading forth mightily those who are bound,
and all who behave rebelliously and dwell in tombs.

In Mark's story, too, we hear how Jesus tells the solitary man to 'go *home* to your friends'; that the man had 'often been *bound* but no one had the might to restrain him'; and that he 'dwelt *among the tombs*'.

The second, similar text, Isaiah 65:1–4, runs:

I was ready to be sought out by those who did not ask,
to be found by those who did not seek me.
I said, 'Here I am, here I am'
to a nation that did not call on my name.
I held out my hands all day long to a rebellious people,
who walk in a way that is not good,

following their own devices;
a people who provoke me to my face continually,
sacrificing in gardens and offering incense on bricks;
who sit inside tombs,
and spend the night in secret places;
who eat swine's flesh,
with broth of abominable things in their vessels;
who say 'keep to yourself, do not come near me'.

The clearest points of contact here are the references in
Mark to the man 'living in the tombs', spending the night
and day in the tombs and on the mountains, behaving
'rebelliously'; the reference to eating swine's flesh; and also
to the populace who, after the miracle, rather surprisingly
beg Jesus to go away. The general context, too, is similar.
Jesus has gone for the first time to this half-Gentile territory, which was regarded as unclean in itself precisely
because of the kind of things detailed in the passage.
Devout Jews were not meant to visit the Decapolis. But
Jesus was 'ready to be found by those who did not seek';
'said "Here I am" to a nation that did not call . . .'

Therefore, Mark has taken two texts – which originally
depicted God appealing to the Jews to abandon their
unclean, Gentile ways – and applied them to Jesus, and his
grace and power to cleanse the madness and defilement
even of the Gentiles themselves. The fact that at the end,
contrary to his usual command to keep silence, Jesus orders
the healed demoniac to tell his friends and neighbours
about it, confirms that he is the one who will bring salvation to the Gentiles, and intimates that he inaugurated,
or at least foreshadowed, their inclusion during his own
ministry.

One conventional feature of the exorcism genre is the use

of names to try to establish superiority over an opponent. So the demons initially name Jesus, just as they did in the exorcism of the demoniac in the synagogue: 'I know who you are, the Holy One of God!' [Mark 1:24]). But Jesus immediately counters by demanding their name in reply, and they have to submit. It is interesting that these Gentile demons use a Gentile mode of addressing Israel's God as 'God Most High' (compare Daniel 3:6; 4:2); whereas the 'Jewish' demons in the synagogue had used a Jewish title, 'the Holy One of God'.[3] The demons know that Jesus has the power to 'torment' them. Matthew's version (8:29) adds 'do not torment us *before the time*' – a reference to the punishment that God was expected to inflict on Satan and his minions in the last days.

Many commentators view the story about the swine rushing into the sea as Mark's adaptation of a folk legend about a Jewish healing in a foreign land: it is not essential to the main story, but it serves to confirm the departure of the demons from the demoniac and their large number. It is a regular feature of exorcism stories that demons fear home-lessness and do not like to be moved about (compare Luke 11:24–26), and their preference for the pigs is explained by that animal's evil associations in Judaism. The association of a Roman legion with a herd of pigs was also no doubt an attractive irony. The fact that the demons ultimately end up in the sea seems appropriate, since it was regarded as a 'chaos', a place of demonic activity. It also makes sense of the demons' request to be sent into the pigs. We are proba-bly not to think of them as being destroyed along with the pigs, but simply as ending up in their natural home.

Meaning for Today

The Church as a whole finds the issue of exorcism extremely difficult. Anyone presenting the symptoms of the Gerasene demoniac today would be rapidly committed for treatment for multiple schizophrenia – and quite rightly. It would be very foolish to do otherwise, or to discount the huge, God-given progress that has been made in our understanding and treatment of mental illness since biblical times. Nor is it un-Christian to observe that God works just as truly – and in general rather more reliably and effectively – through normal medical means as through 'supernatural' ones. Nevertheless, there is a good deal of evidence to show that the ministry of exorcism still has a valid place in treating spiritual and personal disorders, though the reality of 'possession' by external forces remains debatable, and the Church is wise in insisting that the ministry of exorcism should always be complementary, not alternative, to conventional psychiatric medicine.

But as we have seen, personal exorcism is not what this miracle story is really 'about'. Rather, it is about the promise, expressed in the exorcism of the demoniac, of God's ability to defeat and re-order the disordered powers that afflict both individuals and communities – and in this case, their particular expression in war and political violence. In his important studies of the biblical concept of 'the powers that be',[4] Walter Wink analyses the functions of the 'demonic' within human social systems. He starts from St Paul's observation that all the powers, whether conceived of supernaturally or politically, are created and set in place by God with a good purpose (Romans 13:1), but that they become demonic by turning from their God-willed function to serve self-seeking and idolatrous ends. When

this occurs, they generate self-replicating systems of domination and oppression. The unique method of opposing
and ultimately healing them that Christ taught and exemplified is one of non-retaliatory spiritual resistance, which
relies on God's power alone. Since the mechanism of the
powers' domination is always one of threat and violence,
opposition through threat and violence is always to lose out
to the powers, however virtuous or victorious such opposition may seem in the short term. The only truly Christian
form of resistance is prayerful, non-violent witness and
protest – in the firm faith that even the powers, however
warped and fallen they may be, are ultimately creatures of
God, and are ultimately redeemable by his love. One may
temporarily have to submit to the powers in the sense of
suffering their violence, like Christ, even to death; but one
never submits to accepting their warped, self-idolizing
methods and values.

One of the mechanisms by which the powers maintain
their system of domination is by rigidly classifying those
who are included and those who are excluded, those who
are 'friends' and those who are 'enemies'. The profundity of
this miracle story is shown in the fact that Jesus goes out
to heal the very one, the 'Legion', the Gentile, who is the
symbol of the alien oppression. Jesus is shown doing something that in his own day was unthinkable for a devout Jew,
let alone a rabbi. He steps outside the territory of Israel into
'unclean' territory, heals the most untouchable of the
untouchables, and makes him in effect his first apostle to
the other Gentiles. And he does it unambiguously in the
role of God himself, as an enactment of what God (contrary
to all the current religious tradition and supposition) is
really like: a God who combines his unimaginable power
with an unimaginable, all-embracing love; a God who

holds out his arms to people who never wanted him, never asked for him, rebel against him and behave in ways that suggest they would never be interested in him anyway. However, it turns out otherwise. Here, as in so many Gospel stories, it is the least acceptable who turns out to be the most accepting of what Christ has to offer, and becomes his messenger of the same liberation for others.

Where is this reflected as a reality in the Church today? Parts of the Churches of North and South India are currently growing rapidly through its ministry to the Dalits, the 'untouchables'. Although, like other Christian denominations, these Churches' attitude to the inclusion of the Dalits has not always been wholeheartedly equal and without compromise, today serious attempts are being made to atone for the ambiguous attitudes of the past.[5] Despised and rejected by other faiths, Christ and the Church offer the 'untouchables' acceptance and respect, and thus the possibility of self-acceptance and self-respect. They are for the most part extremely poor and can contribute little financially to the Church, which finds it hard to cater for the huge demand for spiritual and practical help that their influx creates. Here, at least, the Church is doing something very close to what Jesus does for the demoniac and for all the 'untouchables' of the healing stories: embodying the love of God for the outcast – and paying the price of doing so. Not surprisingly, converted Dalits, like the demoniac, often become energetic evangelists to others. The Church which has set them free deserves our admiration and all the help we can give.

The Church in our own country remains the preserve of the relatively rich and well educated; it resembles one of the 'powers that be' far more than a counter-culture that might contradict them. When necessary, the institutional Church has usually been ready to sanctify retaliatory violence and warfare by the State. Its own structural life is built on a hierarchical 'domination system' comparable to that of any political state or group. Its effective values, by contrast with its theoretical values, are very much of this world. Of course, the Church will seek to help, defend and speak up for the underprivileged or marginalized, but it generally does so at a distance. The Church of England dispenses charity, issues policy documents and, by virtue of its establishment, delivers parliamentary pronouncements in support of the homeless, street people, the unemployed, urban priority areas, and the rural poor, for example. It agonizes and draws up reports about the underclass and their innumerable social ills. It has argued in favour of justice and generosity for some of the most marginalized, and has recently condemned popular persecution of our two currently most 'untouchable' and hated categories – asylum seekers and paedophiles. Yet it mostly does these things, as it were, from above. It is only rarely able to do what Christ does – what the Church is really for – that is, to embrace and include them. We rarely succeed in making 'them' part of 'us', partly because 'we' simply do not know how to do it, and partly because the ecclesiastical culture cannot contain such a degree of human difference.

Worse, the Church perpetuates its own special kinds of exclusion and oppression, which even the secular powers have learned to abandon. The Church's current fear of the effect of human rights legislation is a shameful irony, which should alert us to the extent to which we have begun to see our very identity as Christians in terms of the rules by which we exclude others. This fearful, ghetto mentality is typical of the world's worst domination systems. In every age, it seems, the Church must define itself by those whom it labels 'outsiders', so that the rest can feel more comfortably 'in'. That instinct to judge and exclude, which earned Jesus' harshest condemnation, makes the Church look to outsiders more like a sanhedrin of the self-righteous than a company of joyful, forgiven sinners, and it is still keeping out just the kind of people whom Jesus wants in.

For Prayer and Meditation

> I am convinced that modern liberal theologians have too easily discarded the idea of trans-personal forces of evil. Instead of trying to fathom what references to evil spirits in the Bible point us to in our own age – which I believe is something quite real – they have dismissed the whole notion of the demonic as implausible. But in my opinion a century that has witnessed Auschwitz and Hiroshima and the Gulag is in no position to laugh off the ugly reality of diabolical forces that seem capable of sweeping people up in their energies.
>
> *Harvey Cox*[6]

The . . . error is to isolate the demonic from its origins in political theology, that is, in the theology of structural sin. . . . It is striking that Black Theology, a movement rooted in the experience of human racial oppression and of the structures of injustice, has rediscovered the true sense of the demonic. Thus one writer comments:

> Already the demons are being named. The enemy is being identified. Its names are legion. Racism is a demon. Poverty is a demon. Powerlessness is a demon. Self-depreciation is a demon. And those who prop them up are demonic in effect. A strategy of liberation

includes a ministry of exorcism, the naming and cast-
ing out of demons.

Kenneth Leech[7]

There is a modern equivalent among the Lunda-Luvale
tribes of the Barotse in what was then Northern
Rhodesia. They always had . . . traditional ailments
called *mahamba*, which resulted from possession by
ancestral spirits. But they then developed a special
modern version called *bindele*, the Luvale word for
'European', which necessitated a special exorcistic
church and a lengthy curative process for its healing.
Legion is to colonial Palestine as *bindele* was to colonial
European Rhodesia, and in both cases colonial exploita-
tion is incarnated individually as demonic possession . . .
Colonial exorcisms are at once less and more than
revolution; they are, in fact, individuated symbolic
revolution.

John Dominic Crossan[8]

The act of praying is one of the indispensable means by
which we engage the Powers. It is, in fact, that engagement at its most fundamental level, where their secret
spell over us is broken and we are re-established in a bit
more of the freedom that is our birthright and potential.
. . . Prayer that ignores the Powers ends by blaming God
for evils committed by the Powers. But prayer that
acknowledges the Powers becomes an indispensable
aspect of social action. We must discern not only the
outer, political manifestations of the powers, but also
their inner spirituality, and leave the Powers, inner and
outer, to God for transformation . . . This is the goal: not

only to become free *from* the Powers, but to *free* the Powers. Jesus came not just to reconcile people to God despite the Powers, but to reconcile the powers themselves to God (Col 1.20). We do not seek to rid ourselves of subsystems and structures in order to secure an individualistic paradise on earth or an afterlife in heaven. We seek rather to relate those systems to the One in and through and for whom they exist, and in whom all things hold together (Col. 1.16–17).

Walter Wink[9]

You have heard that it was said, 'You shall love your neighbour as yourself'. But I say to you, Love your enemies, and pray for those who persecute you, that you may be children of your Father who is in heaven.

Matthew 5:43–45

How can I love my neighbour as myself
when I need him as my enemy –
when I see in him the self I fear to own
and cannot love?

How can there be peace on earth
while our hostilities are our most
cherished possessions –
defining our identity, confirming
our innocence?

Eric Symes Abbott[10]

8

The Raising of Jairus's Daughter and the Healing of the Woman with a Haemorrhage

One of the leaders of the synagogue named Jairus came and, when he saw Jesus, fell at his feet and begged him repeatedly, 'My little daughter is at the point of death. Come and lay your hands on her, so that she may be made well and live'. So he went with him.

A large crowd followed Jesus and pressed in on him. Now there was a woman who had been suffering from haemorrhages for twelve years. She had endured much under many physicians, and had spent all that she had, but rather grew worse. She had heard about Jesus, and came up behind him in the crowd and touched his cloak, for she said, 'If I but touch his cloak, I will be made well'. Immediately her haemorrhage stopped; and she felt in her body that she was healed of her disease. Immediately aware that power had gone forth from him, Jesus turned about in the crowd and said, 'Who touched my clothes?' And his disciples said to him, 'You see the crowd pressing in on you; how can you say, "Who touched me?"' He looked all around to see who had done it. But the woman, knowing what had happened to her, came in fear and trembling, fell down before him, and told him the whole truth. He said to her, 'Daughter, your faith has made you well; go in peace, and be healed of your disease'.

While he was still speaking, some people came from the leader's house to say, 'Your daughter is dead. Why trouble the teacher any further?' But overhearing what they said, Jesus said to the leader of the synagogue, 'Do not fear, only believe'. He allowed no one to follow him except Peter, James and John, the brother of James. When they came to the house of the leader of the synagogue, he saw a commotion, people weeping and wailing loudly. When he had entered, he said to them, 'Why do you make a commotion and weep? The child is not dead but sleeping'. And they laughed at him. Then he put them all outside, and took the child's father and mother and those who were with him, and went in where the child was. He took her by the hand and said to her, 'Talitha Cum', which means, 'Little girl, get up!' And immediately the girl got up and began to walk about (she was about twelve years of age). At this they were overcome with amazement. He strictly ordered them that no one should know this, and told them to give her something to eat.

Mark 5:22–43 (Matthew 9:18–26; Luke 8:41–56)

Commentary

This is an example of Mark's fondness for sandwiching one story within another. The intervening story leaves the necessary time for the situation in the first half of the story to develop towards the climax reported in the second half.

Also, the stories of Jairus's daughter and the haemorrhaging woman have strong thematic similarities linking them together, so that the one illuminates the other. Both emphasize the need for faith; both recount situations that are beyond medical help; both are about women; and both show Jesus touching the 'unclean', overturning the taboos of his own time. Together they form a climax to the section of miracle stories in Mark 4:35–5:43: Jesus' power is shown in a progression from natural disturbance to human illness, and finally to victory over death itself. Some have also seen a kind of progression in the quality of faith shown in these stories. We move from the disciples' faithlessness during the storm, to the demoniac's recognition of Jesus' power, to the haemorrhaging woman's faith in possible healing, to Jairus's faith, which is in effect faith in resurrection.

Let us start with the healing of the woman with a haemorrhage. It was presumably some kind of menstrual disorder that had proved incurable by medical means. It is important to recognize that this would have put her in a constant state of ritual defilement:

This condition would have made her virtually outcast, as she would defile anyone with whom she came into contact, even if they only touched something that she had handled. Every woman would have known what it was to be 'unclean' for one week in the month, but this woman, so Mark tells us, had had a constant flow of defiling blood for twelve years. This might help to explain the stealth with which she approaches Jesus: she was committing an act . . . of defiling a rabbi while he was unaware of her presence. But when challenged she admits her fault; and the fear with which she does so tells us something of her own sense of uncleanness, her expectation that her touch would be disgusting to Jesus. But instead of blame she gets praise for her faith.[1]

Just as the healings of the leper and the Gerasene demoniac implied the inclusion of whole categories of the outcast and unclean, so the healing of the haemorrhaging woman implies a new and startlingly inclusive attitude on Jesus' part towards women. This revolutionary attitude is shown elsewhere in the Gospels by Jesus freely associating with women in a way that would have been thought unconventional, if not shocking, in a Jewish rabbi. But this miracle story is especially important, because in a sense it goes to the heart of the problem. The generally low esteem in which women were held in contemporary Jewish society was strongly conditioned by a menstrual taboo. Menstruation was taken to be the result of God's 'curse' on Eve in Genesis 3:16. The levitical rules laid down that a woman remained unclean for the whole period of her discharge – however long it lasted – and for seven further days following. Uncleanness meant exclusion not only from public worship, but also effectively from normal social life, since every thing and every person she touched also contracted the contamination. This explains the emphasis on touch in this miracle, the woman's terror in daring to approach Jesus; and perhaps also the idea that the healing power flowed even through his garment – corresponding in reverse, as it were, to the way the contamination was supposed to be communicated.

The taboo about a Jewish male touching a female also comes into play in the story of Jesus' healing of Jairus's daughter. The fact that the girl is said to be twelve years old is often thought to have been included in explanation of the fact that she 'got up and walked', since the reader might otherwise imagine she was an infant. A girl of twelve, however, was of marriageable age, which means that by taking her hand Jesus was again overstepping the normal bounds of convention. Nevertheless this is only one, and probably the subsidiary one, of two taboos that are exploded by his action here. Contact with a dead body was also non-kosher, and demanded a similar period of quarantine and ritual washing.

The act of raising the dead is the climax of this series of miracles in Mark, as it is the climax of the Gospel, which in a sense this miracle anticipates (though of course the cases are different: Jairus's daughter, like Lazarus, is raised to normal life and will die again; Jesus is raised to eternal life). It was a standard view in Judaism that God alone had the power to raise the dead. In a contemporary rabbinic proverb, it was one of the three 'keys' in God's hand that he gave to no other – the other two 'keys' being the power to make rain and the power to enable childbirth. Certainly the bystanders have no expectation of such a possibility, which is why, after the girl's death, they tell Jairus to 'trouble the Rabbi no further'; they could believe he might have had power to help when she was still alive, but now that she had died, there was nothing to be done. It is true that others, notably Elijah, had successfully prayed to God for a person to be brought back from the dead, but here there is no mention of Jesus praying. As at the calming of the storm and the healing of the demoniac, Jesus simply does what God does: he acts directly in the person of God himself. It is a supreme demonstration of his identity as well as of his power.

Correspondingly, it is important that these stories illustrate a progression from belief in the power of Jesus to faith in his person. The woman with a haemorrhage clings desperately to a belief in Jesus' supernatural power to heal, which she envisages as a sort of impersonal energy that can be tapped by touch. The Hellenistic world abounded in healing stories of miraculous power, which is viewed in more or less magical terms, and Jesus often shows awareness of the danger of misunderstanding which this involved. The Gospel itself reports that Jesus' own miracles *could* 'work' in that quasi-magical way. In Mark 6:56 we are told that 'even those of the crowd who touched only the fringe of his cloak were healed'. In this story, too, we are told that the 'power' flows from Jesus automatically, as it were, but the mechanism of the healing is then subordinated to a personal confrontation between Jesus and the woman: the healing is only confirmed when Jesus has explained that her *faith* – her response to the person of Jesus himself – is what has made her well. Two points in the narrative tend to confirm this. First, the words 'heal' and 'save' are the same in Greek. Verse 34 can equally be translated 'your faith has brought you salvation; be cured from all your sickness'. Secondly, Jesus now addresses her as 'daughter', implying a personal relationship between them. So here again, the story moves beyond the case of an individual seeking healing from a particular disease at a given time, and becomes symbolic of salvation by faith for all those who find healing and wholeness in the widest sense through entering into relationship with Jesus.

Jairus seems to come close to faith in Jesus from the first. Despite his senior position as leader of the synagogue, and in stark contrast to the actions and attitudes of the other 'rulers of Israel', he publicly falls on his knees before Jesus (the word in Greek is the same as 'worship') and humbly declares his belief that Jesus can heal her. In the second part of the story, although Jesus tells him 'do not fear, only have faith', there is no indication that his faith is in fact failing. It is the rest who try to prevent Jesus continuing; and both parents of the girl are admitted to witness the healing while the others are put outside. The high degree of Jairus's faith is probably related to the magnitude of the miracle. So is the fact that Jesus admits only the inner circle of his own disciples, the same three who witness the glory of his divinity on the Mount of Transfiguration, to be present with the parents. At the Transfiguration they were warned to tell no one of the vision until Jesus had risen from the dead. Here, too, they are ordered to be silent (however impossible that might seem): what is done must be seen only by those who will understand it not as mere wonder-working, but in relation to their own faith in Jesus. Jesus' Aramaic words to the girl have been compared by some commentators to the foreign-language incantations often used by magical healers, but that is clearly not their function here. Rather they imply the opposite, expressing, as in the case of the haemorrhaging woman, a striking degree of personal warmth. His command to give her something to eat similarly introduces a remarkably realistic note of practical human concern, and may also have the function of showing that this is a resuscitation to continued earthly life, not a resurrection to eternal life on the model of Jesus' own.

Nevertheless the resuscitation anticipates resurrection – both Jesus' own and that of the believer. There are many signs in the story of its universal relevance. The same ambiguity we noted in Jesus' words to the haemorrhaging woman also underlies Jairus's prayer to Jesus that his daughter might 'be made well and live'. This might equally be read to mean, 'that she may be saved and attain eternal life'. The words translated 'arise' and 'get up' are the normal Greek words for 'resurrection'. There is ambiguity, too, in Jesus' words, 'She is not dead but sleeping'. 'Sleep' was a common euphemism for death in ancient usage, but was used by the early Christians in a different way to mean the kind of sleep from which one ultimately wakes, and so as a statement of faith in the resurrection. At the symbolic level, then, the raising of Jairus's daughter, albeit to earthly life, prefigures the resurrection to eternal life of all those who have faith in Jesus.

Meaning for Today

As evidence of Jesus' attitude to women, the healing of the haemorrhaging woman can hardly be overstated. In very many cultures and religions menstruation is still super-stitiously understood as a cause of defilement, and as an excuse for the denigration, subjugation or exclusion of women. In the Jewish and Christian religions the pernicious understanding of menstruation as the curse of Eve has been used to justify the worst excesses and abuses of patriarchy, and worse still has contributed to lodging in the minds of countless women a belief in the badness of their own body and the moral inferiority of their sex. In some parts of the Christian Church women are still kept separate from men during worship, and denied Holy Communion during their period. The rite for the 'Churching of Women' in the Anglican Book of Common Prayer bears witness to the continuation of the taboo in our own country until rela-tively recent times. Nor has it disappeared. Astonishingly, it re-emerged in the debate over the ordination of women in bizarre suggestions that at a certain time of the month a woman priest might 'defile' the sanctuary or the sacrament.

It is a grim example of the Church's long ability to discount or neutralize the implications of Jesus' teachings. The healing of the haemorrhaging women is one of many healing stories that demonstrate his will to welcome, embrace and include all the 'non-kosher' categories of people who were officially excluded by the prejudices and taboos of his own society: Samaritans, tax-collectors, lepers, persons with various deformities and sicknesses that rendered them 'unclean' – and women. These were people who, according to Leviticus, were supposed to be literally hateful in God's sight. Instead Jesus declares them to be in God's special care. Just as the healing of the Gerasene demoniac shows Jesus cleansing the 'defilement' attached to the Gentiles and his will to include them in the community of God's children, so this healing shows Jesus throwing aside the irrational fears and inhibitions of his own culture, touching the supposedly untouchable, and welcoming her as God's beloved child. The cruel, irrational taboo about menstruation, with all its dark, destructive implications for women down the centuries, was cancelled in one warm and loving word. Alas, it has taken the Church twenty centuries to notice.

The touching and raising of Jairus's daughter overturns another taboo – about death. This one also remains very powerful in our own culture. It is a cliché that death, not sex, is our current 'dirty word'. Medical advances have prolonged life and the quality of life significantly, with the result that we are less acquainted with serious illness and death as facts of life, and when they come along we are surprised and lack the resources to deal with them. The funeral industry has so taken over the management of death that we scarcely ever see a dead body. Mourning customs have disappeared, and mourning itself has become socially unacceptable, privatized. The process of dealing with death has been removed from the sphere of the family and community to a distant otherworld of professional strangers. Funeral services can last little more than fifteen minutes, and often take place in the surreal, plastic environment of the crematorium. This is all evidence of a growing taboo, the product of a fear that has grown with the fading of faith.

The story of the raising of the girl is meant to reassure us of our own hope of resurrection to eternal life, through faith in Christ. Whether the story is historical fact or literary symbol cannot be objectively shown; and the question seems less important than the one as to whether one takes the promise of our own eternal life to be factual or, as 'non-realist' Christians suppose, only an image of potential for this life. St Paul, writing in a definitely non-symbolic genre, insists that without a real hope in a real resurrection to a real afterlife, the Christian faith is a waste of time (1 Corinthians 15:12–19), and we may well agree with him. But it remains true (as the story itself insists) that it must depend on faith. The nearest thing to certainty that can be obtained in this life grows from the relationship to Jesus to which the miracle itself points as a necessity. And this faith, as both these miracle stories show, means much more than belief. One may 'believe' in a wonder-worker in the sense of assenting to the reality of his powers, in the same way that 'the demons believe in God and tremble' (James 2:19). Belief alone is worth very little, being often indistinguishable from superstition. But New Testament faith, *pistis*, means a relationship of trust, personal commitment, 'faith in' someone, not just 'faith about' them. Finding such a faith in Christ, and discovering that he himself is faithful in return, is what the Gospels call 'salvation' – and provides

the most real reassurance that if he is faithful in this life, he
will remain faithful in the next.

For Prayer and Meditation

Women's impurity is manifest, for Leviticus, in menstruation and in childbirth; and one finds both anxieties
gradually creeping into later Christian practice, with
women barred from receiving Communion during their
menstrual periods and requiring 'purification' after
childbirth. Thus, both single and married women were
automatically suspect of impurity. It was an easy step
from that to feeling that they must be kept well away
from the altar. The result is an ongoing sense among
many Christians that ordination of women simply feels
'wrong'. It is typically a visceral reaction more than an
intellectual one.

William Countryman[2]

When a young girl bleeds in a woman's way,
she refrains from Eucharist
in Ghana, I am told.
When a woman bleeds
on days she is between
the months she is with child,
she cooks and eats her meals apart
because she is defiled,
so several wives for the man you see
are a practical necessity,
a tradition from of old.
Jesus,
the blood of the woman who bled

mingles with the blood you shed,
as a sign of contradiction,
for it has been revealed:
who touches the hem of your justice
absolutely will be healed,
but not without crucifixion.
Now what will it take
to stop the flood
of discrimination
associated with blood?

Miriam Therese Winter[3]

Women play an important role in the Gospel vision of the vindication of the lowly in God's new order . . . The role played by women of marginalized groups is an intrinsic part of the iconoclastic messianic vision. It means that the women are the oppressed of the oppressed. They are the bottom of the present social hierarchy and hence are seen, in a special way, as the last who will be first in the Kingdom of God.

Rosemary Radford Ruether[4]

O God, the power of the powerless,
you have chosen as your witnesses
those whose voice is not heard.
Grant that, as women first announced
the resurrection
though they were not believed,
we too may have courage
to persist in proclaiming your word,
in the power of Jesus Christ. Amen.

The St Hilda Community[5]

Christ our healer,
beloved and remembered by women,
speak to the grief which makes us forget,
and to the terror that makes us cling,
and give us back our name;
that we may greet you clearly
and proclaim your risen life. Amen.

The St Hilda Community[6]

9

The Healing of the Syrophoenician Woman's Daughter

From there Jesus set out and went away to the region of Tyre. He entered the house and did not want anyone to know that he was there. Yet he could not escape notice, but a woman whose little daughter had an unclean spirit immediately heard about him, and she came and bowed down at his feet. Now the woman was a Gentile, of Syrophoenician origin. She begged him to cast the demon out of her daughter. He said to her, 'Let the children be fed first, for it is not fair to take the children's bread and throw it to the dogs'. But she answered him, 'Sir, even the dogs under the table eat the children's crumbs'. Then he said to her, 'For saying this you may go – the demon has left your daughter'. So she went home, found the child lying on the bed, and the demon gone.

Mark 7:24–30 (Matthew 15:21–28)

Commentary

Jesus goes once again into mainly Gentile territory, and is approached by a Gentile woman, asking him to heal her daughter. He has already performed a healing of a Gentile in Mark 5: the demoniac whose 'legion' of demons was sent into the herd of pigs. Here, too, a demon is exorcised (though at a distance), but on this occasion Jesus grants the healing with the greatest reluctance. The most startling aspect of the story for the modern reader is his answer to the woman's request: 'Let the children be fed first; it is not fair to take the children's bread and throw it to the dogs'. Although Mark's account softens the word 'dog' with a diminutive ending ('doggies'!), this is inescapably the standard Jewish insult against the 'unclean' Gentiles. Contrary to modern Christian expectation and all concepts of political correctness, Jesus seems to be endorsing this piece of prejudice, and making it clear that the 'bread' of his mission was intended for the true 'children' of God – the Jews. Although the woman's daughter is healed because of her humility and faith, the impression remains that the grace is given grudgingly, and very much as an exception. In Matthew's version of the story the reluctance on Jesus' part is even greater: when the disciples ask Jesus to send the bothersome woman away, he tells her, 'I was sent only to the lost sheep of the house of Israel'; and the woman is called a 'Canaanite', a term that recalls the Gentiles of the settlement period in Canaan from whom the Israelites were commanded to separate themselves.

There is no question that Mark, Matthew and all the evangelists approved of the mission to the Gentiles and their inclusion in the Church, which was a reality at the time they wrote. This story is a reminder, however, that at best the mission to the Gentiles was always secondary in Christ's purpose to the mission to the Jews. There is no doubt that Jesus accepted the distinction between Jew and Gentile as part of God's plan, and regarded his commission, and that of the first disciples, as being to Israel (cf. Matthew 10:5,6, where Jesus tells them, 'Go nowhere among the

Gentiles . . . but rather to the lost sheep of the house of Israel'). Jesus is likely to have shared the hope that ultimately salvation would come *through* the Jews to the Gentiles – a hope that had been expressed in a number of prophetic texts (Isaiah 19:19–25; 60; 66.19ff.; Zechariah 8:20ff., etc). But this was explicitly a hope for the last days that, as it emerged, was not to be realized until the rejection of Jesus by his own people, and the turning of the post-resurrection mission to the Gentiles. Therefore, though the Gospels of Mark and Matthew record healings of Gentiles, it is emphasized that these were exceptional anticipations of their future inclusion, and did not call into question the difference between Jew and Gentiles, and their relative place in the order of salvation. It is significant that even after the Gentile mission had begun, Paul, the great apostle to the Gentiles, insisted that the election of the Jews as God's first-born children stood firm, and that the proclamation of the gospel was always 'to the Jew first, then to the Greek'. We have also noted that this pattern of salvation is symbolized in Mark's and Matthew's Gospels by the double feeding miracles of the five thousand and the four thousand.

In Mark's story the faith and humility of the Syrophoenician woman is implied in the fact that she recognizes this pattern of salvation, and that it is from Jesus, the Jewish Messiah, that grace is to be obtained. (The Samaritan woman in John's Gospel, whose character may be partly based on hers, also has to accept the same truth [John 4:22].) The fact that in Greek she addresses Jesus as *kyrios* – which could mean 'Mister' or 'Lord – is a further hint that she at least half-recognizes whom she is addressing. In Matthew's version this faith and recognition on her part are made more explicit, as she addresses Jesus as 'Son of David' and 'worships' him, so that Jesus replies to her, 'Woman, great is your faith!' Here the point being made is similar to that of the punchline in the healing of the centurion's servant: 'Not even in Israel have I found such faith'.[1] The irony is that these Gentiles already show a degree of faith which proves lacking in Israel itself – foreshadowing the future general rejection of the gospel by the Jewish people, and the subsequent turning of the Christian mission to the Gentiles. As in the case of the healing at Gerasa, it may also be significant that here, in Gentile territory, there is no command to the woman to keep quiet about the healing miracle.

Luke, perhaps not surprisingly – since he was writing his Gospel for Theophilus, an influential Gentile – omits the story of the Syrophoenician woman altogether, along with its insulting reference to Gentiles as 'dogs', and he removes any suggestion that Jesus was opposed to including the Gentiles in his mission, even during his own lifetime.

Meaning for Today

'How odd of God to choose the Jews', wrote W. N. Ewer in the 1920s, when anti-Semitism was fashionable in Britain.[2] Modern Christians find the idea of Israel's election peculiarly hard to deal with; it appears to counteract all our concepts of justice and racial equality, and to leave God open to the charge of favouritism, or at best, 'counting some more equal than others'. This miracle faces us with God's oddness in a particularly stark way. But before we accuse God of injustice, it is important to consider what election meant. It never meant – at least in the most thoughtful traditions of Israel – that God was supposed to care more about the Jews than anyone else. In the eighth century BC Amos was very clear that Yahweh cared just as much about the Ethiopians and the Cushites as about Israel. In a famous rabbinic commentary on the Exodus, where Pharaoh and his host are drowned in the Red Sea, God is depicted as saying, 'Silence, O Israel: the Lord is not rejoicing, for the Egyptians are also my children' (*Taz* 490: 3; *Sanhedrin* 39b; *Megillah* 10b).

We have to ask the question: if Israel is God's chosen race, *what are they chosen for?* One answer, certainly, is to show forth God's salvation to the whole world, to be the source of the light that would enlighten the Gentiles. 'Salvation is of the Jews', as Jesus reminds the Samaritan woman (John 4:22). But this choosing is not that of a pampered favourite, while the rest must suffer. If anything it is the other way around: Israel is chosen to suffer for the sake of the world, to be the Suffering Servant described by Isaiah through whom salvation comes to the nations (Isaiah 42:1-4; 49:1-6; 50:40-49; 52:13-53:12). It is obviously impossible to understand Jesus himself without understanding his relation to the Jewish people. It is not simply that he is the Jewish Messiah; rather, as the Suffering Servant he embodies the pattern and mystery of Israel's own redemptive vocation, and shows God's own total involvement in it. Almost every detail in the Gospel story relates in some way to the story of Israel as its key. It is as if the whole destiny of Israel is focused in Christ. God chose the Jews not only to suffer for his salvation, but also to show that he suffers too, and that in Christ he can make sense of all suffering by bringing it to resurrection and eternal life.

Most Jews have not acknowledged Jesus as the Messiah. Nevertheless, as Paul says, their election stands: they are still God's first-born children, and the hope remains that one day the old Israel and the new Israel in Christ will each recognize their destiny in the other, and be gathered into one. 'When the full number of the Gentiles has come in, so all Israel will share in salvation'.[3]

For Prayer and Meditation

You only have I known
Of all the families of the earth;
Therefore I will punish you for all your iniquities.

Amos 3:2

Thus says the Lord of hosts: In those days ten men from nations of every language shall take hold of a Jew, grasping his garment and saying, 'Let us go with you, for we have heard that God is with you'.

Zechariah 8:23

Let us pray for the Jewish people,
the first to hear the word of God,
that they may continue to grow in the love of his name,
and in faithfulness to his covenant. . . .

Almighty and eternal God,
long ago you gave your promise to Abraham and his
    posterity.
Listen to your Church as we pray
that the people you first made your own
may arrive at the fullness of redemption.
We ask this through Christ our Lord.

Extract from the Liturgy of Good Friday

Our God and God of our fathers,
Reign over the whole universe in thy glory,
and in thy splendour be exalted over all the earth.
Shine forth in the majesty of thy triumphant strength,
Over all the inhabitants of thy world,
that every form may know that Thou hast formed it,
and every creature understand that Thou hast created it,
and that all that hath breath in its nostrils may say:
The Lord God of Israel is King
and his dominion ruleth over all.

Extract from the Jewish New Year Liturgy

Lord Jesus Christ,
Son of Mary, Star of David,
Light of all the nations, the glory of your people Israel:
we bless you for the Jews, your race, your flesh and
    blood;
we bless you for their faithfulness to you in every age
    and every tribulation;
we bless you for their guardianship of your promises
    and laws;
we bless you for their witness to redemption out of
    suffering,
their living out the mystery of your self-giving love.
Forgive us, Lord, your Church, the iniquities we have
    inflicted on your people,
for making them still a scapegoat for sin -- and in your
    name!
Forgive us the suspicions and the sneers,
the pogroms and the ghettoes,
the exiles and exterminations,
the horrors of two thousand years of wrong.

Take from us, Lord, the taint of prejudice and hate.
Hasten the day of the New Jerusalem,
when we shall all rejoice together to be branches of one
    vine,
sheep of one fold,
children of one Father.
We ask it for your love and mercy's sake. Amen.

Jeffrey John

10

The Healing of a Deaf Mute

Then Jesus returned from the region of Tyre, and went by way of Sidon towards the Sea of Galilee, in the region of the Decapolis. They brought to him a deaf man who had an impediment in his speech; and they begged him to lay his hand on him. He took him aside in private, away from the crowd, and put his fingers into his ears, and he spat and touched his tongue. Then looking up to heaven, he sighed and said to him, 'Ephphatha', that is, 'Be opened'. And immediately his ears were opened, his tongue was released, and he spoke plainly. Then Jesus ordered them to tell no one; but the more he ordered them, the more zealously he proclaimed it. They were astonished beyond measure, saying, 'he has done everything well; he even makes the deaf to hear and the mute to speak'.

Mark 7:31–37

Commentary

This story is not included in Matthew's or Luke's Gospels; but in the corresponding section of Matthew[1] we are given a general list of healings that Jesus accomplished, including 'the mute'. In Mark's Greek the description of the man's affliction is very precise: he is not deaf and dumb, but deaf with an impediment in his speech; this is why, as a result of the healing, he is said to speak *plainly*. The word that renders 'with a speech impediment' (*mogilalos*) is extremely rare, but it appears in the Greek version of the following text of Isaiah 35:5,6, in which the prophet lists the glories of the last days:

> Then the eyes of the blind shall be opened
> and the ears of the deaf unstopped;
> then the lame shall leap like a deer,
> and the tongue of the speechless [*mogilalos*] sing for joy.

The appearance of this word in Mark's miracle story is very strong evidence that, whatever history lies behind it, Mark consciously wrote it to demonstrate that Jesus 'fulfilled' the text of Isaiah 35. In the last verse of the story, when the bystanders refer to Jesus healing the deaf and dumb man, Mark uses the ordinary Greek terms. So it may be that the original healing was of a deaf and dumb person in the 'normal' sense, but Mark has partly changed the detail to make it fit the prophecy in Isaiah 35, which, as we saw in Chapter 1, had a special significance for his theology of revelation.

It is striking that Mark preserves Jesus' use of the Aramaic 'Ephphatha', 'Be opened'. Healers and wonder-workers in Jewish and classical cultures frequently used foreign words and incantations to impress and add an air of mystery. Since Aramaic was Jesus' own language that clearly does not apply to him, but it is possible that Mark kept the Aramaic phrase to heighten the sense of drama or to add verisimilitude. The reported actions of Jesus in healing the man – the laying on of hands, touching the affected part of the body, sighing, looking up to heaven, and the word of command – are also well attested as part of the stock-in-trade of both Jewish and pagan healers in Jesus' day.

There are remarkably strong literary and linguistic links between this miracle and the healing of the blind man of Bethsaida in Mark 8:22–26. The healing of the deaf mute rounds off what is known as the first 'feeding cycle' in Mark – that is, the section after the feeding of the five thousand; and the healing at Bethsaida rounds off the second 'feeding cycle' following the miracle with the four thousand. Both miracles share a striking number of features, some of which distinguish them from the other Gospel healings. They both have the same impersonal beginning ('And they brought to him'). In both there is no mention of demon-possession, nor any mention of the need for faith. In both the afflicted person is taken aside privately. Both involve the use of spittle. In both Jesus looks up to heaven; in both there is a command to secrecy. Finally, both were omitted by Matthew and Luke – perhaps the best explanation being that the later evangelists were embarrassed by their magical-seeming accompaniments.

The conclusion is inescapable that by content, expression and arrangement these miracles are intended to form a pair. The reason for pairing them is to show the double fulfilment of the prophecy in Isaiah 35:5,6: the eyes of the *blind* shall be opened and the ears of the *deaf* unstopped. Mark's special interest in the opening of eyes and ears in Isaiah 35 derives from his general preoccupation with the mystery or hiddenness of revelation – often known as the 'Markan Secret'. We have already seen that at the heart of his perception of that mystery was the text from the beginning of Isaiah, which Mark quotes or alludes to many times. Immediately after Isaiah's vision in the temple and his response to God's call, God had commanded him:

> Go and say to this people:
> 'Keep listening but do not comprehend;
> keep looking, but do not understand.
> Make the mind of this people dull,
> and stop their ears,
> and shut their eyes,
> so that they may not look with their eyes,
> and listen with their ears,
> and comprehend with their minds,
> and turn and be healed'.
> And I said, 'How long O Lord?'
>
> *Isaiah 6:9–10*

It is hardly an exaggeration to say that Mark was obsessed with this passage and the strange theology it contains. Isaiah writes in the near despair of a prophet who knew that he would not be heeded by his people. He burns with the fire of God's message; he is oppressed by the power of the word within him – yet the people seem unable to receive it: they are deaf, blind, hermetically sealed from the Word of God. The more he strains to make them understand, the more they seem unable to hear. Yet Isaiah remains convinced that whatever happens must ultimately be willed by God – even the people's refusal to hear God's message. And so he draws the only possible, but bitterly ironic, conclusion: that in a sense God's word causes the people's blindness and deafness; it only aggravates and points up their inability to hear it. In this text, Isaiah represents God as telling him, at the start of his prophetic commission, to *make* the people deaf, blind and stupid.

God knows that will be the effect of his message; but still the prophet must deliver it.

The early Church had even more reason than Isaiah to feel the tragedy of the people's deafness to God's message. How could Israel have rejected their long-awaited Messiah, their age-old hope and expectation? Inevitably they seized on this theology of unheeded prophecy – which also figures strongly in Jeremiah and Ezekiel – but in particular on this passage of Isaiah, to explain why Jesus himself, as God's ultimate prophet and messenger, had been unheeded and rejected by his own people. This rejection followed the pattern of the past, and they reasoned, like Isaiah, that it must have been intended by God as part of his larger plan. In his anguish over Christ's rejection by his own people, Paul argues, quoting Isaiah 6:9–10, that God must have willed Jesus' rejection by the Jews in order that the gospel might go to the Gentiles, and to allow time for 'the full number of Gentiles to come in'.[2] Mark uses the same text to explain why Jesus was not recognized in his own time; why he himself (Mark says) deliberately obscured his message by speaking in parables,[3] and often ordered those he healed not to speak about it. The same text is used to explain the deafness, dumbness and blindness of the disciples, even after they have been confronted with the most amazing displays of Jesus' power. This unmitigated stupidity of the disciples in Mark (which is usually omitted or softened in the later Gospels) represents the deafness of the old Israel and all humanity, in their constant failure to see, hear and understand the revelation Jesus brings. It is especially noticeable after the two miracles of feeding. After the first, Mark comments, 'they were utterly astounded, for they did not understand about the loaves, for their hearts were hardened' (6:52). After the second, Jesus slams them for their failure to understand about the bread and demands, 'Do you still not perceive or understand? Are your hearts hardened? Do you have eyes and fail to see? Do you have ears, and fail to hear?' (8:17–18).

The healing of the deaf mute and the healing of the blind man of Bethsaida, each closing one of the two feeding cycles, together symbolize the ultimate healing of this spiritual deafness and blindness. In the same way, Isaiah 35 resolved Isaiah 6:9–10 in its description of the last days, 'when the eyes of the blind shall be opened and the ears of the deaf unstopped'. The words of the bystanders at the end of the healing of the deaf mute point to this future as to a new creation – 'he has made all things well' (cf. Genesis 1:31); and it is this future reference that probably explains why, exceptionally, neither of these two miracles mentions the need for *faith*. Faith is certainly needed now, as the one thing that can break through the age-old barrier to communication that separates God and humanity. But these miracles point to the longed-for day when human stupidity and 'hard-heartedness' will be finally healed, the barrier taken away, and when faith itself will pass into knowledge.

Meaning for Today

In the modern Roman Catholic rite of baptism, the priest touches the ears and the mouth of the newly baptized person, and says, 'The Lord Jesus made the deaf hear and the dumb speak. May he soon touch your ears to receive his word, and your mouth to proclaim his faith, to the praise and glory of God the Father.' In the older Roman rite the priest was directed to use his own saliva to touch the ears and mouth, and to shout the words 'Ephphatha! Be opened!' into each ear as he did so. This ancient rite, and the modern prayer which now accompanies it, perfectly express the inner meaning of Mark's miracle, acknowledging as it does that before we can hear the Word of God, we need God himself to open our ears to do so. Our natural state is not one of readiness to hear his message; rather, it is the opposite. Only those who – by God's grace – have ears to hear *can* hear.

The Prophets were in anguish over the people's spiritual deafness. Jesus wept for Jerusalem, 'How often would I have gathered your children together as a hen gathers her brood under her wings, and you would not!'[4] It is still the case that a Christian priest or minister, or any Christian who attempts to share the gospel, is likely to hit the same barrier and share something of the same agony, the agony of God desperately trying to get through to his estranged children. But at the same time we ourselves – as individual Christians, as congregations, as institutional churches – must recognize our continuing resistance to God's message to us, especially when it threatens to challenge and change us. At best we are *selectively* deaf – we will hear as much truth as we imagine we can cope with, and instinctively block out the rest. 'Mankind cannot bear very much reality', as T. S. Eliot observed. But God does not deal in illusions. He will keep pushing to make us hear and see the truth – about him, the world, others and, hardest of all, ourselves – because 'it is the truth that sets you free'.

However we understand the doctrine of the Fall, a large part of its meaning is that we are born spiritually autistic – instinctively self-centred and self-enclosed. In our natural state it is hard for God to break through to us, and for us to break through to him. We need Ephphatha to be shouted in our ears; we need our tongue loosed to be able to pray, praise and tell God's truth freely. And even after contact has been established, we are always in danger of closing in again and shutting him out. It is the work of God's Spirit constantly to batter our hardened hearts, to break through the carapace of fearful self-preoccupation and self-illusion with which we surround ourselves. It is the Spirit who breaks down barriers to make communion between God and people, and between people and people. When the Spirit comes, we cease to be deaf or tongue-tied. We can dare to listen to the promptings of his love, and lose our inhibitions – in the best sense – to risk loving others in turn.

For Prayer and Meditation

Hear him, ye deaf; his praise, ye dumb,
your loosened tongues employ;
ye blind, behold your Saviour come;
and leap, ye lame, for joy!

Charles Wesley, 'O for a thousand tongues to sing'

Sacrifice and offering you do not require,
but you have given me an open ear
[lit. you have dug out an ear for me].

Psalm 40:6

The truth which makes men free is for the most part the truth which men prefer not to hear.

Henry Agar[5]

Batter my heart, three-person'd God; for, you
as yet but knocke, breathe, shine, and seeke to mend;
That I may rise, and stand, o'erthrow mee, and bend
your force, to breake, blowe, burn and make me new.

I, like an usurpt towne, to another die,
Labour to admit you, but Oh, to no end.
Reason, your viceroy in mee, mee should defend,
But is captiv'd, and proves weake or untrue.
Yet dearly I love you, and would be lov'd faine,
But am betroth'd unto your enemie.
Divorce mee, untie, or breake that knot againe,
take me to you, imprison mee, for I
Except you enthrall mee, never shall be free,
Nor ever chast, except you ravish mee.

John Donne[6]

If I say, I will not mention him, or speak any more in his name, then within me there is something like a burning fire shut up in my bones. I am weary with holding it in, and I cannot.

Jeremiah 20:9

Moses said to the Lord, 'O my Lord I have never been eloquent, neither in the past nor even now that you have spoken to your servant, but I am slow of speech and slow of tongue'. Then the Lord said to him, 'Who gives speech to mortals? Who makes them mute or deaf, seeing or blind? Is it not I, the Lord? Now go, and I will be with your mouth and teach you what you are to speak'.

Exodus 4:10–12

All it takes for evil to triumph is for good people to remain silent.

Martin Niemöller

O Lord open thou our lips
And our mouth shall show forth thy praise.

Psalm 51:15

Three Healings of the Blind

1. The Healing of the Blind Man of Bethsaida

They came to Bethsaida. Some people brought a blind man to Jesus and begged him to touch him. He took the blind man by the hand and led him out of the village; and when he had put saliva on his eyes and laid his hands on him, he asked him, 'Can you see anything?' And the man looked up and said, 'I can see people, but they look like trees, walking'. Then Jesus laid his hands on his eyes again; and he looked intently and his sight was restored, and he saw everything clearly. Then he sent him away to his home saying, 'Do not even go into the village'.

Mark 8:22–26

Commentary

The 'Ephphatha' healing of the deaf mute in Mark 5 forms a pair, as we noted in the commentary, with this miracle of the healing of the blind man at Bethsaida. Mark intends both miracles together to show the double fulfilment in Christ of Isaiah's promise: 'the eyes of the blind shall be opened, and the ears of the deaf unstopped' (35:5). Like Isaiah's own prophecy, both miracles are about the healing of people's spiritual, rather than physical, senses. They look to the day when the mysterious barrier to communication between God and his people will finally be torn down.

The unique peculiarity of the Bethsaida miracle is that it happens in two stages. After the first laying on of Jesus' hands, the man sees only dimly – 'I can see people, but they look like trees, walking'. Only after the second attempt does he see clearly. This may be one reason why Matthew and Luke omitted this miracle (another is their possible embarrassment about the magical gestures accompanying it). It might have been seen as implying that Jesus' first attempt at healing the man was not successful because his own powers were somehow insufficient. Mark, however, sees a special significance in the two-stage healing, which is why he has deliberately placed it here, at the centre and turning point of his Gospel.

Mark's Gospel is a drama of revelation in two acts. In the first half Jesus' identity is revealed in his miracles and teaching, yet the disciples in their spiritual blindness still seem unable to grasp the meaning of what they see. But in the middle of the Gospel, at Caesarea Philippi (Mark 8:27ff.), Peter becomes the first to blurt out the truth: 'You are the Messiah'. As soon as the words are out, Jesus begins the second phase of the revelation, explaining to Peter that the Messiah must be condemned and crucified. Immediately Peter rejects this teaching, and is rebuked: 'Get behind me, Satan! You think as men think!' Nevertheless Jesus continues this teaching about the nature of his messiahship and the necessity of the cross through the following chapters, down to its realization in the passion narrative.

The two-stage healing of the blind man of Bethsaida, placed immediately before the dialogue at Caesarea, beautifully mirrors this two-stage pattern of revelation. More specifically, it mirrors the two stages of Peter's personal enlightenment. At this crucial point it reminds us that illumination may be only partial and gradual, but Jesus will continue to open our eyes until we see clearly. In addition to the thematic link there are also structural similarities between the miracle story and the dialogue at Caesarea: both the blind man and Jesus are taken aside by Jesus; both are commanded to secrecy. It is interesting, too, that John's Gospel tells us that Peter himself came from Bethsaida – perhaps a historical reminiscence, or perhaps John's own deduction from perceiving the parallelism in Mark between Peter and the blind man.

2 The Healing of Bartimaeus

They came to Jericho. As Jesus and his disciples and a large crowd were leaving Jericho, Bartimaeus, son of Timaeus, a blind beggar, was sitting by the roadside. When he heard that it was Jesus of Nazareth, he began to shout out and say, 'Jesus, Son of David, have mercy on me!' Many sternly ordered him to be quiet, but he cried out even more loudly, 'Son of David, have mercy on me!' Jesus stood still and said, 'Call him here'. And they called the blind man, saying to him, 'Take heart; get up, he is calling you'. So throwing off his cloak, he sprang up and came to Jesus. Then Jesus said to him, 'What do you want me to do for you?' The blind man said to him, 'My teacher, let me see again'. Jesus said to him, 'Go; your faith has made you well'. Immediately he regained his sight and followed him on the way.

Mark 10:46–52 (Matthew 20:29–34; Luke 13:35–43)

Commentary

It is no accident that the healing of Bartimaeus is the last healing miracle in Mark's Gospel: it is the climax to the theme, which is so important to Mark, of spiritual blindness and sight. It comes at a crucial point, following the last of Jesus' predictions of the passion, and before the entry into Jerusalem and the start of the passion narrative. Jesus' teaching on the nature of his messiahship is now complete, but the disciples are still only half-seeing, as their quarrelling about their own superiority and status in the immediately preceding episode makes clear.[1] By contrast, Bartimaeus *immediately* recognizes the identity of Jesus as Messiah ('Son of David, have mercy on me'), and for the first time in the Gospel this declaration is made without being followed by a rebuke or a call to secrecy. His *faith* is commended by Jesus and demonstrated by his conviction that he can heal him. Jesus declares to him that this faith has *made him well* (or *saved* him: the same word in Greek, as we have seen). He *rises up* and *throws off his cloak* – words that some have seen as alluding to baptism, as an enactment of resurrection and 'putting off' the old life for the new. Finally, and most importantly, the end of the story is that Bartimaeus *follows Jesus in the way*. The phrase strongly recalls the main burden of Jesus' teaching in the preceding section that the would-be disciple of Jesus must *follow in the way of the cross*. Bartimaeus's healing becomes a symbol of Christian conversion and particularly exemplifies the final revelation, which the Twelve were still resisting. Enlightenment is never complete until the disciple learns to serve as Jesus serves, takes up his cross and follows him.

Matthew and Luke also place this miracle immediately

before Jesus' entry into Jerusalem. Matthew, oddly, doubles the number of blind men healed, perhaps in compensation for his omission of the blind man of Bethsaida.

3. The Healing of the Man Born Blind

As he walked along, Jesus saw a man blind from birth. His disciples asked him, 'Rabbi, who sinned, this man or his parents, that he was born blind?' Jesus answered, 'Neither this man nor his parents sinned; he was born blind so that God's works might be revealed in him. We must work the works of him who sent me while it is day; night is coming when no one can work. As long as I am in the world, I am the light of the world'. When he had said this, he spat on the ground, and made mud with the saliva and spread the mud on the man's eyes, saying to him, 'Go, wash in the pool of Siloam' (which means Sent). Then he went and washed and came back able to see. The neighbours and those who had seen him before as a beggar began to ask, 'Is this not the man who used to sit and beg?' Some were saying, 'It is he'. Others were saying, 'No, but it is someone like him'. He kept saying, 'I am the man'. But they kept asking him, 'Then how were your eyes opened?' He answered, 'The man called Jesus made mud, spread it on my eyes and said to me, "Go to Siloam and wash". Then I went and washed and received my sight'. They said to him, 'Where is he?' He said, 'I do not know'.

John 9:1–12

133

Commentary

There is good reason to believe that John's story of the healing of the man who was blind from birth, together with the dialogue following it, represents his own drawing out of the inner meaning of the two healings in Mark, which he has conflated into one story. According to Clement of Alexandria, John's Gospel is a 'spiritual re-working of the things that are obvious to the senses' in the other Gospels, and this is good evidence for that view. That the healing has a primarily spiritual, not physical, meaning is made explicit by Jesus' saying, immediately before he performs it, 'I am the light of the world'. This healing is a 'sign', which like all John's signs finds its true meaning in Jesus himself: it is about the healing and illumination that he offers to everyone. The fact that the man is blind from birth expresses the New Testament understanding – which concurs with the traditional Christian doctrine of 'original sin' – that all are born estranged from God, and until God acts to restore our spiritual vision, and the union with him for which we were originally intended, we remain estranged from him.

There are also allusions to baptism here – as in the story of Bartimaeus, but rather stronger – as the sacramental means of illumination. The context of chapter 9 still seems to be that of the Feast of Tabernacles, as it is in the previous chapter, where Jesus discourses on both water and light, two main themes of the temple ritual for the feast. The blind man is told to wash in the pool of Siloam, from which water was ritually brought to the temple each day of the feast, to the singing of Isaiah 12:3: 'with joy you will draw water from the wells of salvation'. The story makes a point of reminding us that Siloam means 'He who is Sent'. Since there is great emphasis in John on Jesus as the one sent from the Father, it is hard to believe that John did not intend here an allusion to baptism 'into' Christ as the means of salvation and the healing of our spiritual birth-blindness. The best manuscripts of this story also tell us not merely that Jesus 'smeared' the man's eyes with mud, but also that he 'anointed' him, *epichriein*, the word related to 'Christ – Anointed One', from which we derive 'christening'. Whether anointing with oil occurred at baptism in the New Testament period is questionable, but the word 'anointing' was certainly used to describe the work of the Holy Spirit in baptism. Finally, several catacomb paintings show that this miracle was undoubtedly understood in a baptismal sense from at least the second century onwards.

Mark's idea of an enlightenment that comes in stages is also present in John, but greatly elaborated. Reading the whole story through to the end of the chapter 9, the blind man, under repeated interrogation from various by-standers, makes statements that express an ever-deepening understanding of Jesus. At first he knows only that this healer was 'the man called Jesus' (v. 11) Questioning by the Pharisees provokes him to declare that Jesus is a prophet (v. 17). Further pressure brings him to the point of declaring 'He is from God'. Finally, in dialogue with Jesus himself, he declares his faith in him as the Son of Man and worships him (vv. 38,39).

However, at the same time as the blind man grows to faith, his interlocutors in this wonderfully ironic exchange are shown becoming ever more hardened in their own failure to see. Initially, they at least accept the fact of the healing (v. 15). While some are offended by the violation of the Sabbath rules, others seem willing to be convinced (v. 16). Then they begin to disbelieve that he was ever blind at all and summon his parents (v. 18). When they summon him again interest in the truth begins to disappear: they make him repeat the details of the miracle to try to trap him (v. 26), and make it clear that no testimony will make them accept that Jesus is from God (v. 29). Finally the Pharisees simply abuse him and throw him out.

At the end of the tale Jesus says, 'I came into this world for judgment, so that those who do not see may see, and those who do see may become blind'. When some Pharisees bridle at this and ask if he means them, he replies, 'If you were blind, you would not have sin. But now that you say "We see", your sin remains'. It is a case not so much of 'none so blind as those who will not see' as of 'none so blind as those who are sure they see already'.

Meaning for Today

The old Book of Common Prayer service of baptism began with a splendid throwaway line, 'Seeing that all men are conceived and born in sin . . .' The sin in question was 'original sin', the accepted diagnosis of the sickness for which baptism was seen as the prescribed remedy. Such a stark expression of the doctrine, and the term 'original sin' itself, have fallen out of favour today. It was a term that often led to misunderstandings, being equated with inherited guilt, or a negative balance in a heavenly ledger, or else attributed to the process of conception itself, as if it were a sexually transmitted disease (Augustine had come near to saying it was). But when shorn of such misunderstandings, the doctrine of original sin exactly expresses the view of all the New Testament writers: that all human beings, though capable of union with God, are born out of communion with him. It might be better to call it 'original alienation', since sin is now generally taken to refer to sins we commit ('actual' sins as opposed to 'original' in the old vocabulary).

There is no need to take this estranged state to be the result of a historical 'Fall', still less to suppose that the faithless or unbaptized are automatically damned; but the fundamental meaning of 'original sin' still feels like a true diagnosis of our human condition. We feel alone and exiled in a strange, unimaginably vast and otherwise apparently empty universe whose meaning and purpose are not clear to us. The prospect of our own death and the death of those we love seems to make it even more meaningless. The fact of sickness and suffering can sometimes make it feel actively hostile. The power of sin and selfishness in ourselves and in society oppresses us. Yet at the same time we have intimations that there is a meaning to our existence that transcends the physical world. We find it hard to accept that our highest values and experiences of love or beauty are simply reducible to chemical configurations in the brain. Most of us still have an instinct to believe in God, or some kind of personal cause behind everything. But we do not know for sure. We cannot be certain that God isn't just a projection of our own needs and longings, a way of keeping going when it might otherwise all seem pointless. Even when we have the faith to pray, it is often hard, because even as we pray part of us still suspects we may be praying into the void.

This self-enclosure, this existential unrelatedness, is the spiritual blindness and deafness of which Scripture speaks, and it takes the miracle of God's intervention to pierce through it. That is not to say that God had ever left the world completely in the dark. To differing degrees, in every age and every culture people have seen something of his light and reality. But in Christ the fullness of God's light broke into the darkened world, conquered death and offered us a new way of relating to God. He incarnated all that God and humanity can hold in common, sharing the human condition even to the point of sharing in death, demonstrating in the resurrection that when our humanity is reunited with God, death is not the end. That union with God is what he now offers us. The gospel is above all a gospel of restored relationship. United with Jesus through his Spirit dwelling in us, we are restored to our status as God's children; we too are guaranteed victory over death, and begin to share in his eternal life now. The first restoration of that relationship is very appropriately described as moving from darkness to light, the first opening of our spiritual eyes to the light of God's reality and presence with us. The conversion of Saul on the Damascus road was said to be accompanied by a dazzling light which blinded him until he was baptized into Christ, when the 'scales fell from his eyes' and he became able to see again. In baptism the imparting of that new light of spiritual vision is symbolized by the giving of a lighted candle, with the command to 'shine as a light in the world to the glory of God the Father'.

But it is important to see, as Mark's miracle at Bethsaida and John's story of the man born blind both remind us, that enlightenment and conversion are always partial and gradual. Even after we have made what we believe is a total commitment to Christ and have been baptized or confirmed in that commitment, still in this world 'we walk by faith not sight'.[2] 'Faith is the assurance of things hoped for, the conviction of things not yet seen'.[3] Like Peter we may still not fully understand the implications of the commitment we have made – in fact, we are very unlikely to. In particular, like Peter and the other disciples, we will probably be unaware what crosses we will have to bear, or what 'following in the way' may demand from us in terms of service and sacrifice. There are even brands of Christianity that try to deny this aspect of Christ's call altogether, and see God's blessing only in terms of worldly power or success – rather like the disciples who demanded the best seats in the kingdom while Jesus was trying to teach them about service. But as the gospel makes clear, real commitment always means sharing in the cross, and our Christian enlightenment is never complete until we understand that and live by it.

We also have to face the disturbing fact that, as individuals or as a church, we can lose the light of faith or mistake it altogether. In the book of Revelation, St John writes to the church in Laodicea – the rich, complacent, lukewarm church that still thinks it sees, but in reality seems to have turned its gaze on itself:

> You say: 'I am rich, I have prospered, I need nothing'. You do not realize that you are wretched, pitiable, poor, blind, naked. Therefore I counsel you to buy from me gold refined by fire, so that you may be rich; and white robes to clothe you and keep the shame of your nakedness from being seen; and salve to anoint your eyes that they may see.[4]

Such a church, or such a Christian, desperately needs new vision and may frequently pray for new vision – but in fact does not want new vision at all, but only more energy to carry on doing the same old things in the same old way. Real new vision, God's new vision, always brings challenge and change. But if we rule change out beforehand, it negates the prayer.

The greatest danger of all for us and for the Church is the kind of blindness exemplified by the Pharisees. This is the mechanism of the will, so brilliantly dissected for us in John's dialogue, which enables us determinedly not to see the truth when it is unmistakeably presented to our eyes. When the Pharisees saw Jesus healing the sick and offering people freedom and joy, they were so alarmed and jealous for themselves that they condemned him as Beelzebub, the devil. It was this stubborn, blind determination to call darkness light and light darkness which Jesus called the only unforgivable sin. And we must note carefully: this is the special sin of *religious* people, when we get so bound up in our own interpretation of Scripture and tradition, or in preserving our religious institutions and the status quo, that in order to protect them we will be prepared to turn truth, reason, love and justice upside down – all in the name of God himself. It is the syndrome that down the centuries has led so many Christians to suppress their best human instincts in order to torture, persecute and oppress those whose vision differed from theirs, and to claim Christ's sanction for doing it. As Jesus says, if the Pharisees had been truly blind – if they genuinely had no inkling of real goodness – they could not have been blamed; but because they preferred to dress up their own jealousy and prejudice as God's will, their guilt remained. The sin of the Pharisees drove them to crucify Jesus, and it remains the deadliest sin to which the religious are prone; which is perhaps why Jesus warned his own disciples that they must always be on the guard to question their real motives and their real guiding principle:

Your eye is the lamp of your body. If your eye is healthy, your whole body is full of light; but if it is not healthy, your body is full of darkness. Consider therefore whether the light in you is not darkness.[5]

For Prayer and Meditation

Bartimaeus represents us all, for he is blind and 'there are none so blind as those who will not see' . . . Begging, on the edge of life, this blind beggar is a picture of the human race in our alienation from God . . . How appropriate that the Church has adopted the words of Bartimaeus and is not ashamed to use them at the outset of its liturgy – *Kyrie eleison; Christe eleison; Kyrie eleison.*

Michael Marshall[6]

Blind unbelief is sure to err,
and scan his work in vain;
God is his own interpreter,
and he will make it plain.

William Cowper, 'God moves in a mysterious way'

Where there is no vision the people perish.

Proverbs 29:18 (AV)

If the light that is within you is darkness, how great is the darkness!

Matthew 6:23

The darkness is no darkness with you,
but the night is as clear as the day:
to you darkness and light are both alike.

Psalm 139:10

Be thou my vision,
O Lord of my heart,
naught be all else to me
save that thou art;
thou my best thought
in the day and the night,
waking or sleeping,
thy presence my light.

Irish c. eighth century, trans. Mary Byrne and Eleanor Hull

It's a long way off, but inside it
There are quite different things going on:
Festivals at which the poor man
Is king and the consumptive is
Healed: mirrors in which the blind look
At themselves and love looks at them
Back; and industry is for mending
The bent bones and the minds fractured
By life. It's a long way off, but to get
There takes no time and admission
Is free, if you will purge yourself
Of desire, and present yourself with
Your need only and the simple offering
Of your faith, green as a leaf.

R. S. Thomas, 'The Kingdom'[7]

12

The Healing of a Boy with a Deaf and Dumb Spirit

When they [Jesus, Peter, James and John] came to the disciples, they saw a great crowd standing around them, and some scribes arguing with them. When the whole crowd saw him they were immediately overcome with awe, and they ran forward to greet him. He asked them, 'What are you arguing about with them?' Someone from the crowd answered him, 'Teacher, I brought you my son; he has a spirit that makes him unable to speak; and whenever it seizes him it dashes him down; and he foams and grinds his teeth and becomes rigid; and I asked your disciples to cast it out, but they could not do so'. He answered them, 'You faithless generation, how much longer must I be among you? Bring him to me'. And they brought the boy to him. When the spirit saw him, immediately it convulsed the boy, and he fell on the ground and rolled about, foaming at the mouth. Jesus asked the father, 'How long has this been happening to him?' And he said, 'From childhood. It has often cast him into the fire and into the water, to destroy him; but if you are able to do anything, have pity on us and help us'. Jesus said to him, 'If you are able! – All things can be done for the one who believes'. Immediately the father of the child cried

out, 'I believe; help my unbelief'. When Jesus saw that a
crowd came running together, he rebuked the unclean
spirit, 'You spirit that keeps this boy from speaking and
hearing, I command you, come out of him, and never
enter him again!' After crying out and convulsing him
terribly, it came out, and the boy was like a corpse, so
that most of them said, 'He is dead'. But Jesus took him
by the hand and lifted him up, and he was able to stand.
When he had entered the house his disciples asked him
privately, 'Why could we not cast it out?' He said to
them, 'This kind can come out only through prayer'.

Mark 9:14–29

Commentary

We saw that the healing of the deaf mute (the 'Ephphatha'
healing) and the healing of the blind man of Bethsaida form
a pair. Together they point to Israel's (and the disciples')
spiritual deafness, dumbness and blindness, as diagnosed in
Isaiah 6:9; but together they also proclaim the fulfilment
in Jesus of the promise in Isaiah 35:5 that at last 'the eyes
of the blind shall be opened and the ears of the deaf
unstopped'. It is no accident that the only two healing
miracles in the second half of Mark's Gospel, following the
crux of Peter's declaration at Bethsaida, also form a match-
ing pair: the healing of a second deaf mute, and the healing
of the second blind man, Bartimaeus. The repetition of this
theme of blindness and deafness is strongly maintained
through the second half of the Gospel, as the hostility
between Jesus and the Jewish authorities intensifies until
their final condemnation of him; and as the disciples' own
spiritual stupidity and failure to understand Jesus persists

up to their final desertion of him. However, both miracles (this one and the healing of Bartimaeus), while they continue to symbolize the deep spiritual darkness at the heart of the tragedy, are also clarion calls to faithful discipleship, and promise final victory for even the weakest disciple.

This miracle story begins immediately after Jesus, accompanied by Peter, James and John, has descended the mountain of the Transfiguration. The fact that they walk straight into a quarrel between the other nine disciples and the Scribes underlines the return to 'normal life', and to the growing conflict between the powers of God's kingdom displayed in the Transfiguration and the powers of darkness and oppression, personified both by the Scribes and by the demon that afflicts the boy. The descent from the mountain recalls the descent of Moses after the appearance of God to him on Sinai.[1] Both Moses and Jesus return to find people behaving as if they had no faith in God, and both react with indignant fury. The parallel may also explain the otherwise inexplicable fact that the people are said to be 'immediately overcome with awe' when they see Jesus. That was exactly the reaction of the Israelites when they saw the face of Moses, which was still shining with God's reflected glory. Possibly Mark has something similar in mind here – though it is also true that in other parts of the Gospel an unexplained mention of 'awe' on the part of the disciples or of bystanders precedes a new departure or disclosure.[2]

We are not directly told the cause of the conflict between the disciples and the Scribes, but since the boy's father answers Jesus' question we can assume that the debate had been about the exorcism that the disciples had failed to achieve. The father's description of the symptoms of his son's illness makes it sound very much like epilepsy, but he calls it possession by a 'dumb spirit'; and Jesus addresses a 'deaf and dumb spirit' in the exorcism. We might, then, be hearing of two separate ailments; but more probably the original story concerned the healing of epilepsy, and Mark has added the references to the 'deaf and dumb' spirit to fit his theological motive.

Jesus' passionate response to hearing that the disciples were unable (literally 'not strong enough') to cast out the demon is not addressed to the father, nor even to the disciples in particular, but to the whole condition of fallen, blind, deaf humanity. His words recall a number of Old Testament texts expressing God's sorrow, anger and impatience with Israel's faithlessness; though paradoxically their unbelief itself might be seen as testimony to Jesus' identity, since the rabbis themselves had predicted that the Messiah's own generation would be specially marked by lack of faith. There may be a particular link between Jesus' 'How long?' and Isaiah 6:11, part of the passage that is arguably the most influential in Mark's theology. After God has told Isaiah to *make* the people deaf, dumb and blind by the very word of his preaching, the prophet himself responds in anguish, 'How long, O Lord?' But here Jesus speaks rather as God himself, bearing the burden of his people, whose unbelief is the primary cause of his suffering.

The main theological focus in the story is not only on faith, but also on the degree of faith required to overcome the power of evil. It is important to remember that Jesus has already given the disciples authority to cast out demons (6:12), and this is the first time that their power has failed to 'work'. The long duration of the spirit's possession; the detailed description and dramatic violence of the boy's symptoms; the spirit's immediate recognition of Jesus and attempt to fight back, leaving the boy as if dead – all testify, along with the words of Jesus' himself, to the particular difficulty of the case. Nevertheless the failure to cast out the demon remains blameworthy, because it is due to lack of faith. But here the question arises: the lack of whose faith? First, the disciples' faith, clearly. They are the main, though not the sole, object of Jesus' criticism: 'faithless generation' includes the Scribes, the bystanders and the boy's father too. The boy's father is criticized in particular, because sufficient faith is needed not only in the healer, but also in the one requesting the healing (though not necessarily in the recipient of it, as in the case of the paralysed man, or Jairus's and the Syrophoenician's daughters). Even Jesus himself, according to Mark, was *unable* to do more than a few healings in their own home town, because of their lack of faith (though Luke and Matthew change *unable* to *unwilling*).

Hence the importance of Jesus' dialogue with the father. The father shows himself to possess a kind of half-faith similar to that of the disciples, shown especially in his hesitant '*If* you are able to do anything'. Jesus' sharp-sounding reply is ambiguous. His repetition of the phrase 'If you are able!' might imply 'How dare you say to me "If you are able"? Are you doubting my ability to do it?' But it is more likely to mean 'If *you* are able!' – in other words, 'the question whether *you* have sufficient faith is more to the point' – and he assures the man that 'all things are possible to one who has faith'. The man's moving and memorable reply is the real 'punchline' of the whole story: 'Lord, I believe; help my unbelief' (or better: 'Lord, I have faith; help me where faith falls short'). It expresses precisely the lesson we have learned from the disciples' failure: that faith is a variable quantity, and may be insufficient in some circumstances. But at the same time, although it is true that the father's faith is imperfect, his very recognition of its inadequacy and his request for help gain him the gift of his son's cure.

This also illuminates the explanation that Jesus gives to the disciples for their failure: that 'this kind can only come out through prayer'. It is, in effect, the boy's father's prayer to Jesus that fills up the deficiency in his own faith. By recognizing that deficiency, and by praying for help, he allows God in, and acknowledges that God alone is the true source of healing. By contrast the disciples had asked, 'why could *we* not cast it out?' Although Jesus has shared part of his authority and his power with them, they are still pre-occupied with power for its own sake, and still blind to the way of faith as the way of humility, service and the cross. 'Prayer' as Jesus enjoins it is not simply another strategy to add to their technique as exorcists, so as to overcome their failure. Rather it represents a disposition that goes, in a sense, a step beyond faith, or at least, it is an enactment of what faith implies. It is the opposite of self-reliance; a reliance on God which actively seeks his help. (Less reliable manuscripts add 'and fasting' to 'prayer' in this verse, which exactly misses the point, and does, in fact, turn Jesus' advice into a 'technique'.) Prayer is faith put into practice, and only prayer 'works' because it alone lets in the full power of God which no evil can withstand – even, when necessary, to 'move mountains'.[3]

As we noticed in the case of other miracles, not least in the healing of Bartimaeus, there are strong intimations of resurrection underlying the story. We are told that the demon tries to kill the boy by drowning or fire; at the end of the exorcism the boy looks like a corpse, so that everyone says 'He is dead'. But (as with Jairus's daughter) Jesus 'took him by the hand and raised him up'. These are strong hints, counterbalancing the ever-darkening gloom of the second half of Mark's Gospel, that the ultimate victory over 'deafness', all spiritual sickness, the power of evil and death itself, is yet to come.

Meaning for Today

God has the power (if we let him in) to defeat the force of the demonic which, however we understand it, constantly tries to imprison us within ourselves and our fears, and prevents us from hearing and speaking the truth. The work of God is to create communion; as he himself exists as a communion of persons in love, he constantly extends his love to his creation, seeking to draw us in. The work of evil is to create separation, self-centredness, non-communication. Just as the demon convulses the boy, makes him rigid, and leaves him 'as if dead', in our case it straitjackets us in a self-centredness that shuts God and others out, and ultimately leads to personal atrophy and spiritual death. It is a syndrome that threatens every aspect of human life, both individual and corporate.

So this miracle should make us ask questions about our own spiritual deafness and dumbness. In what ways am I deaf to hear what God is trying to say to me? In what ways am I tongue-tied about the gospel, unable to speak about it or show it in my life? What are the demons that oppress and 'deaden' me, and make me 'rigid' through fear, which stop me hearing the truths I resist and speaking the truths that I know I ought to speak?

We need to ask the same about the Church. What are the mechanisms of its own institutional deafness? Where does the demon of fear work corporately to create a culture of non-listening, which in turn makes the Church unable to address those who most desperately need Jesus' message? Where is it colluding with social mechanisms of oppression? Where is Christ's own Body 'convulsed' by internal conflict, or 'rigid' or 'as if dead'? Where is it engaged in a fruitless 'dialogue of the deaf'? Where is it tongue-tied, unable to speak with conviction and authority?

We need to ask the same questions about our society and our world. Where is the power of evil at work, making people incapable of hearing each other? Who are the dumb that are never heard, because they are too powerless to merit attention, or because they are intimidated into silence? Who are the deaf who choose not to hear them? Where does the power of the state, or the power of groups and authorities within the state, operate today to stifle the voices of contradiction? Where is the demonic power that corporately possessed and convulsed Nazi Germany or Stalinist Russia working in the world today, and where is it raising its head?

The battle against the demonic inside us and outside us can only be won by a faith that issues in prayer. It is a huge battle on all three fronts. To confront and combat the personal demons that isolate and oppress us can be long, hard work. To confront and combat the Church's deafness and dumbness can be disillusioning and exhausting. To confront and combat the forces of the demonic in social and political life always requires courage, and sometimes a literal martyrdom. If we imagine that we can fight any of these battles in our own strength we will fail, as the disciples failed. It needs prayer, and everything that prayer implies. Prayer itself creates communion, and allows the power of the divine communion to flow into the world and into ourselves. The mere act of prayer tears us away from our self-regard and makes us look to God – breaking the circle of our frightened self-centredness, which is the main-spring of the demonic power. That does not mean that prayer is a substitute for action, or an excuse for refusing to change ourselves, or the Church or the world. Both prayer and our own willingness to act, where we can, are neces-sary. What Jesus said to the boy's father he says to us: 'If *you* are able – it is your own will and your own faith that are in question, not mine!' As we grow in prayer, two things happen. First, we are 'conformed to the mind of Christ' – that is, taught to see more and more as God sees, and to pray in conformity with his will, rather than with our own desires. Secondly, we will often be shown things that we ourselves have the power to change; and as long as we keep praying, the Spirit will keep pushing us to change them.

But we have to be realistic, both about what we are up against and about ourselves and the feebleness of our faith. Our self-centredness is so ingrained, and the power of the demonic is so subtle, that we will constantly find ways to turn even our prayer life into new kinds of selfishness or self-enclosure, shutting God out again. However strong we imagine our faith and prayer to be (and especially when we imagine they are strong), it is then we most need to remember that they are never going to be strong enough – and to pray, with the boy's father, 'Lord I have faith; help me where faith falls short'.

For Prayer and Meditation

Truly I tell you, if you say to this mountain, 'be taken up and thrown into the sea', and if you do not doubt in your heart, but believe that what you say will come to pass, it will be done for you. So I tell you, whatever you ask for in prayer, have faith that you have received it, and it will be yours.

Mark 11:23–24

Perhaps your own faith is feeble. Nevertheless, the Lord who is love will stoop down to you, provided only you are penitent and can say sincerely from the depths of your soul, 'Lord, I have faith. Help me where faith falls short'.

Cyril of Jerusalem, Catechetical Lectures 5:9

To intercede is to bear others on the heart in God's presence. Our own wantings have their place, for it is clear from the teaching of Jesus that God wants us to tell him of our wants. When however we do this 'in the name of Jesus' we learn to bend our wantings to our glimpses of the divine will. Intercession thus becomes not the bombardment of God with requests so much as the bringing of our desires within the stream of God's own compassion . . . The compassion of God flows ceaselessly towards the world, but it seems to wait up the co-operation of human wills. This co-operation is partly by God's creatures doing the things which God desires to be done, and partly by prayers which are also channels of God's compassion.

Michael Ramsey[4]

The Lord said to me, 'I am the foundation of your praying. In the first place my will is that you should pray, and then I make it your will too, and since it is I who make you pray, and you do so pray, how can you not have what you ask for? . . .

152

Our Lord is greatly cheered by our prayer. He looks
for it, and he wants it. By his grace he aims to make us as
like himself in heart as we already are in our human
nature. This is his blessed will. So he says, 'Pray in-
wardly, even if you do not enjoy it. It does good, though
you feel nothing, see nothing. Yes, even though you think
you are doing nothing. For when you are dry, empty, sick
or weak, at such time is your prayer most pleasing to me
though you find little enough to enjoy in it. This is true of
all believing prayer'.

Julian of Norwich, The Revelations of Divine Love, ch. 41

Each time you take a human soul with you into your
prayer, you accept from God a piece of spiritual work
with all its implications and with all its cost – a cost
which may mean for you spiritual exhaustion and darkness, and may even include vicarious suffering, the Cross.
In offering yourselves on such levels of prayer for the
sake of others, you are offering to take your part in the
mysterious activities of the spiritual world; to share the
saving work of Christ . . . Real intercession is not merely
a petition but a piece of work, involving costly self-
surrender to God for the work he wants done on other
souls.

Evelyn Underhill[5]

And those whom we, through ignorance or forgetfulness
or the number of names, have not remembered, do thou
O God, remember them, who knowest the age and the
name of each one, who knowest each from their womb.
For thou, O God, art the help of the helpless, the hope
of the hopeless, the saviour of the tempest-tossed, the

harbour of mariners, the physician of the sick. Be thou thyself all things to all, who knowest each, their dwelling and their need.

The Liturgy of Basil the Great

Pray as if everything depended on God, and work as if everything depended on man.

Joseph Spellman

13

The Healing of the
Centurion's Servant

When Jesus entered Capernaum, a centurion came to him, appealing to him and saying, 'Lord, my servant is lying at home paralysed, in terrible distress'. And he said to him, 'Shall I come and cure him?' The centurion answered, 'Lord, I am not worthy to have you come under my roof; but only speak the word, and my servant will be healed. For I also am a man under authority, with soldiers under me; and I say to one, "Go", and he goes, and to another, "Come", and he comes, and to my slave "Do this", and the slave does it'. When Jesus heard him, he was amazed, and said to those who followed him, 'Truly I tell you, in no one in Israel have I found such faith. I tell you, many will come from east and west and will eat with Abraham and Isaac and Jacob in the kingdom of heaven, while the heirs of the kingdom will be thrown into outer darkness, where there will be weeping and gnashing of teeth'. And to the centurion Jesus said, 'Go; let it be done for you according to your faith'. And the servant was healed in that hour.

Matthew 8:5–13 (Luke 7:1–10; John 4:46–53)

Commentary

There are distinct similarities between this healing story and the story of the healing of the daughter of the Syrophoenician woman (in Mark) or Canaanite woman (in Matthew). In each case Jesus is approached by a Gentile on behalf of another, beloved person who is not present; Jesus, as a Jew, shows some reluctance to respond to the request, but the Gentile shows such humility that Jesus acquiesces, fulfils the healing and praises their faith. Jesus' reluctance in the case of the centurion is suggested by the question 'Shall I [as a Jew] come to heal him?' It is possible to translate the Greek phrase simply as 'I shall come to heal him', making Jesus grant the request immediately, but the majority of commentators punctuate the phrase as a question. Even so, the degree of reluctance on Jesus' part is much less than in the case of the Syrophoenician woman.

The centurion himself, despite his request, seems in fact almost more hesitant than Jesus. He is surprised by Jesus' suggestion that he should *come* and see the sick servant in person, because he knows that by 'coming under his roof' Jesus would make himself unclean in terms of the purity laws. His humble and unquestioning acceptance of the distinction of Jew and Gentile is similar to that of the Syrophoenician woman. The centurion, however, shows a remarkable degree of faith in Jesus in two further respects. First, he assumes that Jesus is quite able to perform the healing at a distance, simply by 'speaking the word' – which of course is what happens. Secondly, he makes a very significant comparison between his own authority over the soldiers under him and the kind of authority that Jesus possesses over the power of sickness. He immediately perceives exactly what the Scribes refused to see in the healing work of Jesus. They had called Jesus 'Beelzebub, the prince of demons', attributing to Jesus a superior power of evil, committing an unpardonable blasphemy.[1] The centurion instinctively recognizes Jesus' authority as the 'Stronger One' who is able to bind the evil powers, and perhaps even his *divine* authority: again, like the Syrophoenician woman, he addresses Jesus as *Kyrie*, a word that in secular use might mean no more than 'Sir', but which here carries more than a hint of divine lordship. This instinctive recognition recalls the similar reaction of the centurion at the foot of the cross, 'Truly this man was the Son of God' (Mark 15:39; Matthew 27:54), and probably links with the tradition recorded in Acts that the very first Gentile convert to Christ was also a centurion.

There is remarkably little interest in the physical healing of the servant, which remains invisible and at a distance. As in so many miracle stories, the greater healing to which the story points is the healing of a barrier by the inclusion of a hitherto excluded and despised group. That inclusion cannot be shown happening fully within Jesus' own ministry. Jesus remains the one 'sent only to the lost sheep of the house of Israel', and it is significant that in Matthew's Gospel Jesus never steps into Gentile territory, nor in this story does he in fact enter the centurion's home. The Gentile healings, like the story of the Magi that begins Matthew's Gospel, are anticipatory: they point ahead to the Gentile mission after Jesus' resurrection, and at the same time they underscore the irony that whereas the Jewish Messiah found rejection among his own people, he would find faith and welcome among foreigners.

This is also a story of inclusion in one or two less obvious respects. The centurion represents not only the Gentiles, but also the occupying army of Rome. Because of the region's peculiar troublesomeness, and what amounted to an ongoing guerrilla war against various groups of Zealot terrorists, the Roman army in Palestine adopted very brutal methods. Roman soldiers, like the tax-collectors who worked under their supervision, were not surprisingly the objects of deep popular hatred. But as we have seen, the hatred of the occupation had a theological as well as a political dimension. From the time of Daniel onwards, the military forces occupying Israel had been viewed theologically as the visible counterpart of Satan's host: they were the earthly arm of the 'principalities and powers'. The book of Revelation very clearly expresses this understanding of the Roman Empire as the earthly manifestation of celestial powers hostile to God and his people. The conversion of the centurion therefore represents not only the inclusion of the Gentiles, but also the beginning of the inclusion of the invisible powers, the 'spiritual forces of evil in the heavenly places', which had always oppressed God's people and combated God's will. It is an extraordinary irony that the centurion at the foot of the cross, who symbolizes the first Christian conversion, was literally one of the 'rulers of this age who crucified him', but was one whom the cross itself immediately 'vanquished and disarmed'.[2] The faith of the centurion anticipates a literally cosmic 'inclusion': even the fallen powers in earth and heaven can be, and shall be, embraced and redeemed in Christ.

The second aspect of inclusion is more tentative, but it is particularly important for the Church's current wrestling with the 'gay issue'. A first-century Jewish reader of Matthew's or Luke's Gospels would have been likely to conclude that the relationship between the centurion and his servant was more than merely professional. The word

Matthew uses for the sick 'servant' is *pais*, which can mean 'servant', 'son' or 'boy'. Luke uses both *pais* and *doulos*, the regular word for 'slave'. The implication is that he was a domestic orderly. Homosexuality was portrayed by Jews as an exclusively Gentile interest, and the charge of homosexual practice, especially directed against the occupying forces, formed part of conventional anti-Roman polemic in contemporary Jewish literature. The charge was well founded: there is plenty of evidence about Roman military life to back it up.

Domestic 'servants' were often kept by officers on this basis, and some relationships proved famously durable (the emperor Hadrian and Antinous being perhaps the best-known couple). In this story the centurion's deep concern, and particularly the statement in Luke's version that the servant was 'very dear to him', would greatly strengthen a contemporary reader's suspicion (Gerd Theissen brings out the likely Jewish reaction to the story in the piece quoted in the passages for meditation below). The probability that the relationship was homosexual would not have escaped Jesus, Matthew or Luke, and in view of Jesus' systematic inclusion of so many other categories of person who were declared to be 'unclean' or 'abominable' under the levitical rules, it is a real question whether we are meant to see Jesus deliberately 'including' homosexuals here as another category of the despised. Certainly there is no sign of anything but approval on Jesus' part for the centurion and his remarkable faith, nor any hint of 'Go, and sin no more' after his servant is restored to him.

Meaning for Today

It is important not to miss the extent to which the centurion in this story represents the foreigner, the oppressor, and worse. For Jesus' contemporaries the centurion was a creature with supernaturally evil connotations, as well as being a symbol of all-too-real, earthly barbarism and cruelty. It was not for nothing that for three centuries Gentile soldiery had been thought of among Jews as beasts, subhumans or limbs of the devil. When Jesus so warmly commends the centurion for his faith, it is as if a survivor of Auschwitz has commended a Nazi kommandant. Yet for Jesus the weight of inherited group hatred counts for nothing. His immediate welcome of the man is an instance of his constant refusal to approach or judge people as members of a class, race, sex or category of any kind, but only as an individual. He deals with the human being, ignoring the label, and this is the heart of Jesus' 'inclusivity'. To the consternation and disgust of others, he is completely non-tribal and prejudice-free.

However, the lesson to be drawn from this is not simply that we should 'take others as they are and all will be well'. All will not so easily be well, because the powers of group self-interest are not so easily tamed. Jesus approached individuals as individuals; that is the start of the solution, but it is not the end. The processes of tribalism are so ingrained in us that to challenge them is always to risk one's own exclusion and to court hatred from all sides. The centurion remains a paradoxical figure. The centurion at the cross who first proclaims Jesus to be the Son of God may well have been one of those who drove in the nails. The centurion whose servant was healed may well have been another, 'acting under orders'. Most of those who ran the Nazi extermination camps counted themselves as Christian, family men, 'acting under orders' from their superiors, but they were also acting under the compulsion of an evil set of complex circumstances which helped them suppress their conscience and their humanity. The mechanism of corporate domination and prejudice relies on intimidating the members of one's own group as much as the outsiders. Many who, for example, have attempted to cross the sectarian divide in Ulster have paid a heavy price of ostracism, exile, violent punishment or death. Obeying one's conscience in such circumstances can prove too costly. Most of us know how the same mechanism operates in less dramatic ways, silencing us when we should speak out, making us toe the wrong line, keeping us within the wrong boundaries.

Part of the disgust that many Jews would have felt for this centurion and his particular request is the disgust that many heterosexual men can feel for the homosexual. But again with Jesus the disgust does not appear. The servant is healed, and the relationship between the two – whatever it is – is restored. If such acceptance on Jesus' part is one of the lessons of this passage, it has never yet been learned by the Church. Disgust and prejudice in the face of homo-sexuality are still prevalent in today's society, especially in the Church, and they are maintained by the same mecha-nisms of group intimidation. One bishop attending the 1998 Lambeth Conference, which condemned homosexual relationships as 'unscriptural', spoke afterwards of the 'atmosphere of a Nuremberg rally' and an 'air of palpable evil' which hung over the assembly as the vote was taken. Many bishops voted with the crowd and against their con-science because they feared reprisals in their dioceses. Ironically, some attempts were made during the conference to 'exorcise' homosexuals. The truth is that the 'demonic' forces in the genuinely biblical sense were more obviously at work in the assembly.

In this miracle story Jesus commends the faith and meets the need not only of a political enemy and a member of an unclean race, but of one of the very 'rulers of the present age' who put him to death. It was, Paul says in Colossians 2:15, the 'rulers and authorities' – meaning both the visible powers and the supernatural forces that stand behind them – that nailed Jesus to the cross. And yet it was on the cross that Jesus also 'disarmed the rulers and authorities, making a public example of them'. On the cross Jesus 'tricked the powers'. How? By refusing to play the game of group prejudice. By refusing to be deflected from the path of right by terror, even by torture and death. By refusing to hate in turn, and by refusing to retaliate. Above all, by determinedly, patiently and persistently loving even the warped, lying, vicious powers that work in humankind, by loving them to the bitter, bloody end, until he loves them from enemies into friends, and into what they were created to be.

For Prayer and Meditation

Lord, I am not worthy that thou shouldst come under my roof, but speak the word only and my soul shall be healed.

Prayer before Communion, English Missal

The crusading mind is rooted in intolerance, and its ultimate end is destruction of its opposition. The crucified mind is rooted in the love which grows deeper through pain, and which seeks its end through what may seem a harsh and dreadful love, but whose aim is the transformation of its opponents. It is this mind which is expressed so often in the writings and speeches of the late Martin Luther King, and nowhere more powerfully than in his letter of May 1963 after the children's march. He wrote:

> We must say to our white brothers all over the south who are trying to keep us down: We will match your capacity to inflict suffering with our capacity to endure suffering. We will meet your physical force with our soul force. We will not hate you. And yet we cannot in good conscience obey your evil laws. Do to us what you will. Threaten our children, and we will still love you. Say that we are too low, that we are too degraded, yet we will still love you. . . . We will wear you down by our capacity to suffer and still to love. In winning the victory we will not only win our freedom. We will so appeal to your heart and your conscience that we will win you in the process.
>
> *Kenneth Leech*[3]

[Gamaliel, a Jewish teacher who disapproves of Jesus, in dialogue with Andreas, the narrator, says:]
'One day a Gentile centurion living here in Capernaum came to him. He asked him to heal his orderly. Of course you have to help Gentiles. But why this one? Everyone knows that most of these Gentile officers are homosexual. Their orderlies are their lovers. But Jesus isn't interested in that sort of thing. He didn't ask anything about the orderly. He healed him – and the thought didn't occur to him that later someone might think of appealing to him in support of the view that homosexuality is permissible.'

'Are you certain that the centurion was a homosexual?'

'Of course not, but everyone must have their suspicions. Jesus wasn't at all bothered. I would have advised
more caution'.

Gerd Theissen[4]

You are not like us
we are the normal ones
you are the deviant
we are the powerful ones
you have no real power;
if you try to be like us
we may accept you
– but that depends on us
and on how deviant you are.
Don't ever say your way is as valid as ours
we might get worried
we might attack
in fact – *We are who we are*
because you are not who we are.

Harvey Gillman[5]

God, we believe; we have told you we believe . . . We have
not denied you; then rise up and defend us. Acknowledge
us, O God, before the whole world. Give us also the right
to our existence!

Radclyffe Hall

Father of all mercies and giver of all grace, we commend to you these your servants, N and N, who desire your help and guidance for the new life which they begin together this day. Grant them the grace of love and forbearance; grant them your pure and peaceable wisdom to enlighten them in all perplexities, and the power of your Holy Spirit in their hearts to keep constant their trust in you and in one another; through Jesus Christ our Lord.

Jim Cotter, Rite for Blessing a Same-Sex Partnership[6]

We are tempted to think that the chief Christian sufferings should be those inflicted by the world upon the Church, as we rather naively think, by the 'wicked' upon the 'good'. Those sufferings however are easy to bear compared to the peculiar sufferings we bear as Christians within the Church. The Church is where the tensions of human life have to be confronted at their deepest level.

Eric Symes Abbott[7]

Those who work for change suffer resistance.
So make us strong.
Those who do new things sometimes feel afraid.
So make us brave.
Those who challenge the world as it is arouse anger.
So grant us inner peace.
Those who live joyfully are envied.
So make us generous.
Those who try to love encounter hate.
So make us steadfast in you.

The St Hilda Community[8]

14

The Healing of the Man at Beth-Zatha

After this there was a festival of the Jews, and Jesus went up to Jerusalem. Now in Jerusalem by the Sheep Gate there is a pool, called in Hebrew Beth-Zatha, which has five porticoes. In these lay many invalids – blind, lame and paralysed [waiting for the stirring of the water; for an angel of the Lord went down at certain seasons into the pool, and stirred up the water; whoever stepped in first after the stirring of the water was made well from whatever disease that person had]. One man was there who had been ill for thirty-eight years. When Jesus saw him lying there and knew that he had been there for a long time, he said to him, 'Do you want to be made well?' The sick man answered him, 'Sir, I have no one to put me into the pool when the water is stirred up; and while I am making my way, someone else steps down ahead of me'. Jesus said to him, 'Stand up, take your mat and walk'. At once the man was made well, and he took up his mat and began to walk. Now that day was a Sabbath. So the Jews said to the man who had been cured, 'It is the Sabbath; it is not lawful for you to carry your mat'. But he answered them, 'The man who made me well said to me, "Take up your mat and walk"'. They asked him, 'Who is the man who said to you, "Take it up and walk"?' Now the man who had been healed did not know who it was, for Jesus had disappeared in the crowd that was there. Later Jesus found him in the temple and said to him, 'See; you have been made well! Do not sin any more, so that nothing worse happens to you'. The man went away and told the Jews that it was Jesus who had made him well.

John 5:1–9 (Mark 3:1–6; Luke 13:10–17)

Commentary

It is possible to visit the site mentioned in this miracle (near St Anne's Church, to the north-east of the temple area in Jerusalem), where a pool with five porticoes answering the description was excavated in the 1960s. The same pool is clearly mentioned in the Qumran Scrolls, though there is some confusion about the name – different manuscripts of John's Gospel variously call it Bethesda, Beth-Zatha or (probably by confusion with the town) Bethsaida. There is manuscript disagreement, too, about the explanation, given in square brackets in the text above, of the angel stirring the water. This appears only in a few later manuscripts, and seems to be an addition. However, since the man's statement 'I have no one to put me in the water when it is stirred up' makes no sense without some such explanation, the textual addition may represent a genuine tradition, or is at least a good guess. The story of the angel and the pool's healing powers probably arose from the phenomenon of an intermittent spring.

The central chapters of John's Gospel are related to different festivals of the Jewish year (John 6:4 = Passover; 7:2 = Tabernacles; 10:22 = Dedication; 11:55 = Passover again). It is possible to show that the content of these sections relates to the theme of each festival, and in particular to the passages of the Pentateuch which were prescribed for the synagogue readings. There is a very obvious thematic connection between the miracle of Jesus feeding the five thousand and Passover in chapter 6, and a probable one between John's account of the healing of the blind man and the feast of Tabernacles in chapter 9. The festival mentioned at the start of this story is unnamed, but it is a plausible suggestion that it was the Festival of the New Year. The theme of the festival – judgement and a new start – certainly fits the story of the man at Beth-Zatha, and a strong connection can be shown between the New Year festival readings and the discourse on judgement that follows the miracle in the rest of chapter 5.[1]

We are not told what the man's ailment was – we assume lameness or paralysis because of his inability to walk. A number of commentators have criticized the man's dullness, on the grounds of his having attempted the same feat fruitlessly for 38 years, his failure to realize what Jesus could do for him, and even after his healing his failure to identify him until the later meeting. This evidence of the man's hopelessness may help explain Jesus' otherwise seemingly unnecessary question, 'Do you want to be made well?' Jesus seems to want to elicit at least some spark of will on the man's part to be cured. It is an open question whether at the end of the story the cured man reports Jesus to the Jews through stupidity or malice. His action may continue the portrayal of his dullness, or it may be an example of 'Johannine irony', since Jesus has just told him 'do not sin again'.

Some commentators, reading the story symbolically rather than literally, link the miracle with baptism, and relate Jesus' question with the liturgical demand that opens many ancient liturgies of baptism: 'What do you want?' Certainly the story was understood to be symbolic of baptism at least from the second century onwards. However, the fact that water ultimately plays no part in the man's healing, but rather is shown to be quite unnecessary to it, seems to undermine this interpretation fatally. A more plausible symbolic interpretation is that the water stands for the Law, 'which while it may point the way to life and salvation cannot impart the will to choose life, still less impart life itself'.[2] In the story of the wedding at Cana the water also stood for the old dispensation, awaiting its transformation by Jesus. Along similar lines, the five porticoes have been related to the Pentateuch, the man's 38 years of sickness to the 38 years of Israel's fruitless wanderings in the desert,[3] and even the angel to the angels who according to tradition mediated the law to Moses. Such allegorizing may seem far-fetched, but we have already seen plenty of evidence that weaving allusions in this way is not untypical of the Gospel genre, especially in John. Other elements in the story hint at healing in the wider sense of salvation. As in other cases I have noted, the man's first word to Jesus, *Kyrie*, may simply be rendered 'Sir', but it is equally translatable as 'Lord'. *Egeire* means 'stand up', but also 'resurrect'. *Hugies* means 'whole' in the sense of 'well' or 'healthy' but also that of 'holy'. The strongest reason, however, for seeing an image of the passage from old covenant to new in this miracle is the contrast between the man's long, near-despairing wait for a doubtful salvation by very precarious means, and the immediate effectiveness of Jesus' presence and command.

At first sight Jesus' warning to the man to 'sin no more in case something worse happens to you' seems to contradict his teaching elsewhere (John 9:3 and Luke 13:1–5) that there is no link between personal sin and sickness. There need not be a contradiction, however. Clearly sin and sickness are linked in the sense that both are symptoms of human fallenness. When Jesus simultaneously forgives and heals the paralytic lowered through the roof, both follow from the victory of Jesus over the power of evil, through to the faith that restores the man's relation to God. What Jesus denies in John 9:3 and Luke 13:1–5 is any *direct*, *causal* link between personal sin and sickness. Jesus' warning here to the man has to be taken in a more general sense, comparable to his warning to the woman taken in adultery.[4]

Jesus' command 'Stand up, take up your mat and walk' is exactly the same as his command to the paralysed man in the Synoptic story, and may well derive from it, but here the focus of John's interest is very different. Here the emphasis is not on Jesus' authority to forgive sins, but rather his authority to heal on the Sabbath. In this respect the story more closely resembles Mark's account of the healing of the man with a withered hand on a Sabbath, after which the Pharisees and Herodians begin to conspire to get rid of him;[5] and also Luke's account of the healing of the woman who had been crippled for eighteen years, which leads directly into a protracted dialogue with the Pharisees about healing on the seventh day.[6] Like John's story of the healing of the blind man, which gathers up and explores the themes of the Synoptic stories of Bartimaeus and the blind man of Bethsaida, this too seems to be a kind of 'portmanteau' miracle which welds together elements of these others.

As in the Synoptics, it is Jesus' infringement of the Sabbath law that in John's scheme first brings him into serious dispute with the Jewish authorities and opens the conflict that leads to his death. The basis of the dispute is well attested. The 'tradition of the elders' specified thirty-nine categories of work that were forbidden on the Sabbath; the thirty-ninth was to carry a load from one dwelling to another – and it was this one that the man violated by taking up his bed. Jesus' view, as presented both in the Synoptic Gospels and in John, was that the Sabbath was a blessing and not a burden from God. To 'do good' on the Sabbath therefore fulfilled, and did not contravene, God's will; to refuse to do good on the Sabbath actually thwarted God's will. The conflict over Jesus' Sabbath healings presents in its sharpest form the blindness which confuses the letter of the law with the spirit, and refuses to see, in the sheer good of the healings, the authority of the healer himself. This element of blindness is further brought out in John's story of Jesus healing a blind man on the Sabbath in chapter 9, and the dialogue with the Pharisees which follows it.

In Mark, Jesus declares that 'the Son of Man is Lord even of the Sabbath'[7] – with the ambiguity that the 'Son of Man' may refer to himself, or to humanity in general, since 'the Sabbath was made for man, not man for the Sabbath' (see above, pp 36–37). But John's Jesus takes the argument about Jesus' authority still further in the discourse following this miracle, and here there is no ambiguity. Jesus explains that God is still in his own period of 'Sabbath rest' following creation, yet is still working in the world every day. So Jesus says, 'My Father is still working, and I also am working', and his hearers draw the obvious implication: 'they sought all the more to kill him, because he was not only breaking the Sabbath, but was also calling God his own Father, thereby making himself equal to God'.[8]

Meaning for Today

It is not always the case that God needs a sign of faith or will on the part of a person to effect healing. In the healings of the centurion's servant, Jairus's daughter, the Syrophoenician woman's daughter and the paralysed man at Capernaum, the faith is not their own but on the part of people close to them. But in the case of the man at Beth-Zatha, there is no mention of faith at all, either on his own part, or on anyone else's. Perhaps the most striking feature of this man's description is his statement, 'I have no one to help'. After thirty-eight years of isolation and frustrated hope it is not surprising if he seems (in C. H. Dodd's words) rather 'feeble and unimaginative'![9] If faith is too much to ask of a man so near to despair, Jesus at least succeeds in eliciting a still-existing will to be cured, though the man's response shows that he places no particular hope in Jesus, except that he might carry him to the water at the time the angel next disturbed it. After the healing, he still shows little interest in Jesus, and does not even learn his name. At their final meeting there is still no hint of faith or thanks, and in the end, for whatever cause, he betrays him.

This sober realism contrasts with the pattern that characterizes most of the healing miracles: faith called forth; healing accomplished; and praise duly rendered. The picture of the man – whose illness is undefined – despairingly slumped in a portico day after day without any lively hope of change, could be replicated in innumerable shop doorways in most Western cities. The difference is that in most modern cases, the sickness is not physical at all, but is socially or psychologically generated, and usually aggravated by addiction to drugs or drink. But spiritually the end result is the same; precisely what strikes and scandalizes the 'normal' passer-by is the lack of motivation or self-respect in so many people who seem to have chosen this way of life, with no apparent need to do so. They have embraced a short-cut to the same sickness of the will which physical sickness took thirty-eight years to generate in the man at the pool. It is extraordinarily difficult to help, not least because the act of helping confirms the person's belief in his or her own helplessness and self-rejection. Anyone who has tried to support a friend who is locked into one of so many forms of slow self-destruction – alcoholism, addiction, anorexia, suicidal depression – knows the anguish of trying to bend one's own will to bolster another's, and finding the attempt usually counterproductive. The heart of the problem is always Jesus' question: Do you *want* to be made well? No one can answer that question on another's behalf. Such hope as lies in this story is in Jesus' ability to call forth the man's will to be healed, even if it is still locked into the form of the superstitious half-hope he has been clutching for years. As long as some chink of human will remains, God can get in to open the door. But as the sequel to the story suggests, even after God has literally worked miracles in a human life, old patterns can re-establish themselves and push him out again.

As for the conflict about the Sabbath that connects this story to the drama of Jesus' destruction, it is worth asking over which issues today Christians blind themselves, allowing the relatively trivial things of religion itself to negate 'the weightier matters of the law: justice, mercy, and faith'.[10] Denominational differences and strife? Quarrels about prayer books, liturgies and ceremonials? Clashes between religious tradition and social change? The tying down of religion to national and tribal identities? Concerns about Sunday observance itself in some communities? In all these areas and very many more, genuinely religious people always run the risk of focusing down their sights, forgetting God who is always in the larger picture – and, if we are not careful, performing actual injustices and cruelties, fooling ourselves, like the Pharisees, that they are done in his name.

For Meditation and Prayer

Nothing in the world – indeed nothing even beyond the world – can possibly be conceived which could be called good without qualification except *a good will*.

Immanuel Kant, *Foundation of the Metaphysics of Morals, I*

In magnis et voluisse sat est.
In great endeavours to have the will is all it takes.

Propertius, Elegies II, 10.1.5

All sin tends to be addictive, and the terminal point of addiction is what is called damnation.

W. H. Auden[11]

They say you were victorious
Over hell and over death.
We know the hell of heroin,
The dying that is meth.
So come down, Lord, from your heaven,
You whom we can't confess,
And be the resurrection
Of this, our living death.

Stephen Delft[12]

In the course of my work I have met many people who are suffering from terrible disabilities – mentally handicapped people who know they are not as clever as most people, people whose brains and spines have been damaged beyond repair, people who are dying slowly of multiple sclerosis or cancer – and who have not despaired. They know the implications of their disability, but they are able, in a sense to escape from the prison of their damaged body, to separate themselves from their physical pain, and so be interested in life, to care for other people, and to laugh. But in depression no such separation of the body and the free mind is possible. Body and mind are imprisoned, and the pain cannot be transcended. This is why depression is such a terrible affliction.

Dorothy Rowe[13]

I gradually began to think of my depression in new terms. Instead of looking for its causes and thinking how to get rid of them, I began to look for its purposes and to wonder how I could fulfil them. I couldn't and still can't tell whether God sends us such acute afflictions to bring us to some new understanding through our pain. But I am now as sure as I can be that depression is often a sign, whether human or divine, that the life of the victim needs to be drastically changed; that acts of genuine contrition are called for; that the dark blocks within can be dissolved only by recognizing that something like an inner death and resurrection is demanded by the sufferer.

Philip Toynbee[14]

You blind guides! You strain out a gnat and swallow a camel!

Matthew 23:24

Conventionality is not morality. Self-righteousness is not religion. To attack the first is not to assail the last. To pluck the mask from the face of the Pharisee is not to lift an impious hand to the Crown of Thorns.

Charlotte Brontë

15

The Samaritan Lepers

On the way to Jerusalem Jesus was going through the region between Samaria and Galilee. As he entered a village, ten lepers approached him. Keeping their distance, they called out, 'Jesus, Master, have mercy on us!' When he saw them, he said to them, 'Go and show yourselves to the priests'. And as they went, they were made clean. Then one of them, when he saw that he was healed, turned back, praising God with a loud voice. He prostrated himself at Jesus' feet and thanked him. And he was a Samaritan. Then Jesus asked, 'Were not ten made clean? But the other nine, where are they? Was none of them found to return and give praise to God except this foreigner?' Then he said to him, 'Get up and go on your way; your faith has made you well'.

Luke 17:11–19

Commentary

This story is peculiar to Luke, though there are similarities to Mark's miracle of Jesus healing the leper, which Luke has also included at 5:12–16 – in particular Jesus' order to the lepers to go and show themselves to the priests in keeping with the levitical command. The Greek of this story is very distinctively in Luke's style, and many commentators believe it represents Luke's own expansion of the Markan story to incorporate the theme that interests him most: the contrast between the responsive, grateful Samaritan and the unresponsive, ungrateful Jews. Luke is particularly interested in the Samaritans. Of the Synoptic Gospels only Luke reports that Jesus extended his mission into Samaritan territory, and it is only Luke who gives us the story of the Good Samaritan, which similarly contrasts the compassion of the 'foreigner' with the heartlessness of the Jewish religious leaders who 'pass by on the other side'.

The Samaritans, who were descendants of Israelites and Gentile settlers from the Assyrian period in the eighth century BC, had been a thorn in the side of the Jews ever since. They did not undergo the 'purification' of exile in Babylon, and from around the fourth century BC they had set up on Mount Gerizim in Samaria a centre of worship that was a countertype and rival to the temple in Jerusalem (the Samaritan woman in John 4:20 brings this up as the focus of difference). So from a Jewish point of view Samaritans were doubly unclean and beyond the pale: they were both racial half-breeds and religious apostates. (Hence the Samaritan woman's astonishment at Jesus' asking her for a drink [John 4:9].) When Jesus says, 'was no one found to give praise to God except this foreigner?', the word translated 'foreigner', *allogenes*, has a religious as well as racial reference: the historian Josephus tells us that it was the word used in the inscription on the barrier in the temple warning non-Israelites not to enter; it implies 'a religious alien'.[1]

Josephus also mentions that Jews crossing Samaritan territory were often subjected to harassment and sometimes to violence, and no doubt the same happened to Samaritans in Jewish territory. It may be surprising that Luke's story depicts a group of Samaritans and Jews travelling together, though one could reason that since leprosy would have made them outcasts from both communities they might have found common cause in adversity. Luke notes that the lepers 'kept their distance'. As we saw in the discussion of Mark's leper, the reason for this was not only the risk of infection, but also religious contamination: the purity laws in the levitical code laid down strict rules about quarantine, and the need for lepers to give warning to others to keep away.

As it stands the story has some puzzling features. Jesus directs all ten lepers to go and show themselves to the priests in Jerusalem in order that the priests could inspect the lepers, certify the cure and readmit them into the community. That order could not in any case have applied to the Samaritan; and it is odd that the nine who did what they were told are in effect blamed for doing so. Why did the Samaritan have to return to Jesus to offer thanks to God, and why does Jesus assume that the other nine did not offer thanks, especially since a visit to the priests in Jerusalem to certify a cure would generally have involved a thank-offering too? And why, since all ten were cured, is only the Samaritan told that his faith had saved him?

These illogicalities at the literal level of the story are often attributed to carelessness on the part of Luke, but at the level of Luke's theological purpose they are easily accounted for. While it was true that God cleansed the lepers, it was important that it was God acting through Jesus. Jesus is more than a mere instrument here: for Luke, as much as for Mark or John, he is the embodiment of God's own presence and authority. God had acted in him to cleanse the lepers, and in him God must be acknowledged and thanked. It is the Samaritan's prostration before Jesus and his recognition of God's grace specifically working in him that makes Jesus say, 'Your faith has saved you'. And although it is true that all ten were cleansed, for the Samaritan alone these words have their full spiritual as well as physical meaning: 'your faith has brought you salvation' – faith has brought him into a new relationship with God and his kingdom in Christ.

But the sharp point of the story is that only this foreigner has seen and understood. In this it resembles not only the story of the good Samaritan, but also all those in which some category of outsider shows a response of faith or love which 'exceeds that found in Israel' – the Syrophoenician woman, the centurion, the woman of the streets, the tax-collector. It is another foretaste of the opening of the kingdom not only to Gentiles, but also to all outsiders, whose very awareness of being on the outside is what enables them to enter with faith and thanksgiving.

Meaning for Today

Thankfulness goes a step further than faith. One oddity of Luke's story of the ten lepers is that they all must, to some degree, have had faith. Certainly all ten recognized Jesus' authority and begged him for healing, and all ten were healed. But only one was thankful. Faith is only the beginning of relationship: it expresses belief and trust in its object. Often, as in the case of the lepers, it arises out of awareness of a need, and awareness that the person in whom one has faith can supply that need. And that is not despised by Jesus. All ten lepers had at least got that far – further than most of Jesus' respectable and acceptable compatriots. Although it is still self-seeking, Jesus still commends faith. At least it has its eyes open; it is realistic in a way that the spiritually blind are not; at least it recognizes where its need can be met.

But thankfulness, at least when it is real, spontaneous and not calculating, is not born of need; it does not look to itself, but to the giver. The instinct to give thanks is the second half in the circle of relationship that faith begins. In response to the gift being given or the need being met, the receiver wants to give something back, even if it is only praise, appreciation or gratitude. We teach children to say thank you at first by rote, but we do it because we hope that the habit will grow into an instinct, a spirit of real thankfulness. We know that without that spirit the person the child becomes will not develop into a right relationship with those around; he or she will not learn genuine 'give and take' but risks becoming self-centred (in George Bernard Shaw's memorable phrase, 'a feverish, selfish little clod of ailments and grievances, complaining that the world will not devote itself to making you happy'). Many of us who are given to self-preoccupation and pessimism have had reason to thank friends and spiritual advisers for dinning into us the plain, old-fashioned trick of concentrating on thanksgiving in our prayers: 'Count your blessings, name them one by one, and it will surprise you what the Lord has done.' It works. The act of will that forces itself, however grudgingly and reluctantly at first, to list reasons for thanksgiving, most often in the end creates thanksgiving and restores spiritual health, precisely because it tears one's focus away from self to God or others.

In his analysis of the 'Four Loves', C. S. Lewis gave the highest place to 'charity' or *agape* – God's own kind of love, disinterested in the sense that it is essentially selfless, a love that gives itself by its own nature for the good of the beloved. By a paradoxical kind of grace God enables human beings to share in this kind of love – paradoxical because this too, of course, is a gift from him. At our best we are, as it were, able to reflect back to him the self-forgetting kind of love with which he loves us. This kind of love, which is above all the love we will know in heaven when we have 'lost ourselves to find our real selves in Him', Lewis calls 'Appreciative Love':

> God can awaken in man, towards himself, a supernatural Appreciative Love. This is of all gifts the most to be desired. Here, not in our natural loves, nor even in ethics, lies the true centre of all human and angelic life. With this all things are possible.[2]

The spirit of thankfulness is at least one of the lower slopes of Appreciative Love. In this life no doubt it is always mixed with a degree of selfish motive, or of what Lewis calls 'need-love' or natural love. Nevertheless it already contains something of eternity, precisely because it is an aspect of God's own nature, shared with those whom he made in his image.

Thankfulness felt towards God is very close to the spirit of praise and worship (it is interesting that the Samaritan leper in effect comes back to prostrate himself in *worship* to Jesus as well as to thank him). The Appreciative Love of heaven will not be thankfulness to God so much for what he has done as for what he *is* – 'we give thanks to thee for thy great glory'. As the etymology of worship implies – 'worth-ship' – it is a response to perceiving something of the 'value', the overwhelming reality of his being.

Scripture speaks of the worshipper's 'sacrifice of praise' or 'sacrifice of thanksgiving', but it is not a sacrifice in the sense that praise and thanksgiving mean 'giving something up' that is one's own. The spirit of praise and thanksgiving is itself received as a gift, and the giving back is not loss but joy, not diminution but increase. It is one aspect of the mystery of love that makes us more truly ourselves the more we give ourselves away.

The greatest expression of this mystery in the Christian life is the Eucharist (which is simply the Greek word for 'Thanksgiving'). In the Eucharist, God in Christ continues to give himself to us, as he gave himself to us in the Incarnation and on the cross. These saving events are re-presented and made actual to us, and at the same time we are gathered into them, through our incorporation in him. As we receive the Body of Christ in the sacrament, we are confirmed and empowered as his Church, his body on earth. By grace we too are united, in all our imperfection, with Christ's own sacrifice, his great thanksgiving to the Father. We are drawn into the life of the Trinity itself, the eternal cycle of love whereby the Father constantly gives himself in and through the Son, and the Son, gathering all up in himself, is constantly given to the Father. By him and with him and in him, our poor offering of praise and thanks is taken up; it is accepted and sanctified in that one, eternal, perfect self-offering of Christ to the Father. Then, even as we join in that offering, we receive back new life again, the life of God Christ physically, tangibly given us in the Body and the Blood.

Evelyn Underhill's poem 'Corpus Christi', part of which is quoted below, catches something of this tremendous mystery of God's sacrificial love flowing to and from creation, enacted and realized in the Eucharist, through which we too are drawn into the eternal cycle of giving and receiving. As Austin Farrer reminds us in another passage on the same theme, it is against this background of Christ's own great thanksgiving in the Eucharist that all our little causes of thanksgiving, with all their mixed motives, must be set. Through our small responses to daily instances of God's love, we catch and reflect glimpses of the vast, inexpressible love that creates, sustains and redeems us; and as we do so, God willing, we gradually grow in the practice of Appreciative Love, until we are fit to know its consummation in heaven.

For Prayer and Meditation

What is your main reason for thankfulness to the person (let us say) who has been so tolerant as to marry you? Why, that very fact: their willingness to have you, and to go on putting up with you. But then, how your general appreciation of your attitude springs to life at some single, and it may be quite trivial expression of it! It may be a small thing; but it sends you back to your amazement at having so kind a husband or wife. It is not like a surprise act of politeness from a stranger; it is John's or Mary's way: it is characteristic. Now, it is the same with the mercies of God. He has done for us infinite and inexpressible things: he has called us into being: he has redeemed us with sweat, blood and tears. He has placed us in relation to him, as children to a parent; he has promised us everlasting life, and the sight of his face. Yet all these great things often come home to us in little things: in recoveries of sickness; in overcoming difficulties; in successes and occasions of pleasure. These things, small in themselves, bring home to us the infinite kindness of God, and in giving thanks for them, Christians put them on the background of the great mysteries of

religion. In offering the Eucharist, we think it no frivolity
or profanation to thank God for the mercies of daily life.
The little mercies bring the great mercies alive to us: the
love that died for us is the love that blesses our daily
path.

How shall I repay the Lord for all his benefits to me?
I will receive the cup of salvation, and call on the name
of the Lord.

Austin Farrer[3]

When upon life's billows you are tempest-toss'd,
When you are discouraged, thinking all is lost,
Count your blessings, name them one by one,
And it will surprise you what the Lord has done.

Johnson Oatman, Jr

Thou that hast giv'n so much to me,
Give one thing more: a gratefull heart.
See how thy beggar works on thee
By art.

He makes thy gifts occasion more,
And sayes, If he in this be crost,
All thou has giv'n him heretofore
Is lost . . .

Wherefore I crie, and crie again;
And in no quiet canst thou be;
Till I a thankfull heart obtain
Of thee:

Not thankfull, when it pleaseth me,
As if thy blessings had spare dayes:
But such a heart, whose pulse may be
Thy praise.

George Herbert: 'Gratefulnesse'[4]

The worst moment for an atheist is when he feels grateful
and has no one to thank.

Wendy Ward

This is the true joy in life: being used for a purpose,
recognized by yourself as a mighty one, and being a force
of nature, instead of a feverish, selfish little clod of
ailments and grievances complaining that the world will
not devote itself to making you happy.

George Bernard Shaw

Then I, awakening, saw
A splendour burning in the heart of things:
The flame of living love, which lights the law
Of mystic death that works the mystic birth.
I knew the patient passion of the earth,
Maternal, everlasting, whence there springs
The Bread of Angels and the life of man.
Now, in each blade
I, blind no longer, see
The glory of God's growth: know it to be
An earnest of the immemorial Plan.
Yea, I have understood
How all things are one great oblation made:
He on our altars, we on the world's rood.

Even as this corn,
Earth-born,
We are snatched from the sod,
Reaped, and ground to grist,
Crushed and tormented in the Mills of God,
And offered at Life's hands, a living Eucharist.

Evelyn Underhill, 'Corpus Christi'[5]

16

The Withered Fig Tree

Next day, when they returned from Bethany, Jesus was hungry. Seeing in the distance a fig tree in leaf, he went to see if he could find anything on it. When he came to it, he found nothing but leaves, for it was not the season for figs. He said to it, 'May no one eat fruit from you again' – and his disciples heard it.

Then they came into Jerusalem. Jesus entered the temple and began to drive out those who bought and sold in the temple, and he overturned the tables of the money-changers and the seats of those who sold pigeons; and he would not allow anyone to carry anything through the temple. And he taught them, saying to them, 'Is it not written, "My house shall be called a house of prayer for all the nations"? But you have made it a den of robbers'. And the chief priests and the scribes heard it and sought a way to destroy him. They were afraid of him, because all the multitude was astonished at his teaching. When evening came they went out of the city.

In the morning, as they passed by they saw the fig tree withered away to its roots. And Peter remembered and said to him, 'Master, look! The fig tree which you cursed has withered'. And Jesus answered, 'Have faith in God'.

Mark 11:12–22 (Matthew 21:18–22)

Commentary

On the face of it, the story of the withered fig tree casts Jesus in a pretty poor light. One New Testament commentator has described it as 'irrational and revolting . . . lacking any sort of moral motive or justification'.[1] It is certainly unreasonable to demand ripe figs from any and every fig tree that happens to cross one's path, especially when, as the Gospel explicitly tells us, it was not even the season for figs! In cursing the tree so roundly, with words that seem to imply 'If I can't get anything from you, neither shall anyone else', Jesus sounds worse than petulant; and the act of shrivelling it up looks like a mean-minded piece of super-natural vandalism. When it is read at this level, the story recalls some of the most awful tales in the Apocryphal Gospels – in particular one in the *Infancy Gospel of Thomas* which has probably been influenced by it, where the child Jesus, in irritation with a playmate, literally shrivels him up with the words 'you shall wither like a tree and bear neither leaves nor root nor fruit!'[2]

As always, however, to read the Gospel at level of biography or psychology misses the point, which is essentially theological. The clue to the deeper meaning lies in the story of the cleansing of the temple, which separates the two halves of the fig-tree story. As in the case of Jairus's daughter and the haemorrhaging woman, Mark uses the 'sandwich' device partly because it is a means of letting the pattern and meaning of one story shed light on the other. In this case the connecting theme is Jesus' condemnation of the religious system of his own day – dramatically enacted both in the act of cleansing the temple and in the withering of the fig tree. The point is that Israel has not produced the spiritual fruits expected of it, and now the time of judgement has come. The apparently bizarre statement that 'it was not the season for figs' actually points us to this interpretation. The word used for 'season' is *kairos*, the word regularly used in the New Testament to mean 'the opportune time', the time of God's visitation or of his final 'harvesting' of his people.

Why a fig tree? Fig trees and vines frequently go together in the Old Testament to make a proverbial symbol of plenty and peace. The prophetic promise that 'everyone shall sit with their neighbour under their own vine and their own fig tree' is found in slightly different forms in Isaiah, Micah, Zechariah and Joel. Conversely, several prophecies of doom forecast the blasting of the vine and fig tree and the failure of their fruit. There is one particular passage, however, in which the double image of the vine and the fig tree together symbolizes the people of God themselves, and even more particularly their failure to produce the fruit of righteousness at the time of the Lord's visitation:

When I would gather them, says the Lord,
there are no grapes on the vine,
no figs on the fig tree.
Even the leaves are withered,
and what I gave them has passed from them.[3]

This verse was part of Jeremiah's prophecy to Judah at the time when the Babylonians were threatening invasion, while still the people remained complacent and careless in their attitude to God and his law, and the priests falsely preached 'Peace, Peace'. It is hard to believe that this text was far from Mark's mind as he wrote, since the story of the fig tree shows it literally coming true. Now, as he enters Jerusalem for the last week of his life, the Lord himself, God in Christ, has indeed finally come and visited his people in person. Not only does he fail to find the fruits of righteousness in them, but their rejection of him will mean the passing of his blessing from them to others: 'even what I gave them has passed from them'.

If we ask what has happened to the vine in Jeremiah's double image, the answer appears in Mark's next chapter, in the parable of the vineyard and the tenants. Here exactly the same situation reappears. The Lord seeks the fruits of his own property, but receives none. Instead his emissaries are mistreated and killed, and in the final visitation by the Lord's own son, he too is mistreated and murdered. Accordingly, the tenants themselves will be destroyed and the vineyard handed to others – 'what I gave them has passed from them'. The parable is elaborated with reference to a further collection of prophetic texts in which Israel is likened to a vineyard, most famously by Isaiah:

The vineyard of the Lord of hosts
is the house of Israel,
and the men of Judah
are his pleasant planting;
and he looked for justice,
but behold bloodshed;
for righteousness,
but, behold, a cry![4]

For Mark, then, the fig tree and the parable of the vineyard and the tenants are telling the same story, and together they provide a fulfilment of the Jeremiah text about God visiting his people and finding them fruitless. Some scholars, feeling the kind of embarrassment I described at the start about Jesus destroying the fig tree, have suggested that perhaps the fig-tree story itself was also originally a parable, which somehow got changed into a miracle story in the process of transmission. That is possible, but the explanation is unnecessary. The truth is that the Gospel writers simply do not make the same clear-cut distinctions that we try to make between what Jesus did and the stories he told. What matters is that in him the promises and prophecies of the Old Testament come true – whether it is in what he says, or does, or is. Mark would not have worried that the act of Jesus withering the fig tree suggested he was petulant or irritable. That kind of novelistic character-portrayal which is normal to us does not come into his thinking. Rather he would have understood Jesus' withering of the tree as a 'sign' in the tradition of the Old Testament prophets (*oth* in Hebrew) – that is, as an action, which may be 'miraculous' or otherwise in terms of the laws of nature, but which enacts the deeper truth that it symbolizes. (In the classical prophets these prophetic 'signs' are often striking to the point of being bizarre – for instance, Hosea's chaotic domestic arrangements, designed to express Israel's unfaithfulness to Yahweh; or the extremities that Ezekiel is required to undergo as a sign of what Yahweh will do to the house of Israel.)

The non-miraculous cleansing of the temple, to which the fig-tree story is so closely tied, is an exactly similar sort of sign, thoroughly within the prophetic mould. Just as the fig-tree story fulfils the prophecy of the Lord's visitation as described in Jeremiah, this story fulfils two more expectations of the same kind, one from each of the last two books in the Old Testament. The prophet Malachi had predicted that in the last days

the Lord whom you seek will suddenly come to his

temple; the messenger of the covenant in whom you delight, behold he is coming, says the Lord of hosts. But who can endure the day of his coming, and who can stand when he appears? For he is like refiner's fire and like fuller's soap; he will sit as a refiner and purifier of silver, and he will purify the sons of Levi and refine them like gold and silver, till they present right offerings to the Lord.[5]

Even more precisely, the very last words of Zechariah's prophecy (written probably around three centuries before Christ, at the start of the Greek occupation of Israel) looked forward to the day when not only the vessels and accoutrements of the temple would be regarded as holy, but when all the vessels and accoutrements of all the people would be holy – in other words, when personal holiness might become an attribute of the nation's whole life, and not merely a matter of ritual attaching to the temple. In a final sarcastic aside, which shows that the conducting of venal activities in and around the temple was already a problem, the prophet adds: 'And there shall no longer be a trader in the house of the Lord of hosts on that day'.[6]

Pretty clearly, by doing what he did, Jesus was acting out the fulfilment of both prophecies. A number of commentators have expressed puzzlement about the exact focus of the criticism, since the trading that went on at the temple was necessary to its functioning. The animals sold were the animals prescribed for the offering according to the law; and the money changers had to be present because ordinary money was held to be unclean (it bore the emperor's image and violated the second commandment, and so it had to be changed into special kosher money to pay the priests). One can imagine, however, that around these activities there was room for profiteering and doubtful practice, and the Zechariah text suggests that these may have been a long-standing object of discontent and suspicion from pious Jews. Alternatively, the criticism may have been of the *place* where the trading went on, which was in the court of the Gentiles, well outside of the temple building itself. This suggestion is reinforced by Jesus' quotation of Isaiah, in which the prophet had foreseen the inclusion of all nations into the worship of Israel: 'my house shall be called a house of prayer for all nations'.[7] The fact that the one place where Gentiles were allowed to share – very marginally – in the worship of the temple was also the place taken over by traders and moneychangers may well have been seen by Jesus and others as something of a scandal.

Here, however, we hit a problem. Jesus' action in 'cleansing the temple', and his quotation of Isaiah's prophecy about the inclusion of the nations, seem to imply that Jesus believed the temple would continue. His action does not make sense if he knows that in fact it is going to be destroyed. Yet in Mark 13:2 Jesus will be shown predicting the destruction of the temple, and in 14:58 he will be accused at his trial of having said he would 'build another in three days, not made with hands' – implying the temple of his risen body, identified with the Church. Here there seems to be a clash between, on the one hand, what Jesus himself did and meant, and, on the other hand, the evangelist's later interpretation of it. John's version of the story removes the difficulty by simply omitting the prophecy about the temple becoming a place of prayer for all nations and, substituting Psalm 69:9 – 'Zeal for thy house will consume me'. He then adds, as a direct statement of Jesus, 'Destroy this temple and in three days I will raise it up'. In John 2:13–22, therefore, what was originally an act of 'cleansing' – a symbol predicting the temple's reformation – becomes not a 'cleansing' at all, but unambiguously a threat: a symbol predicting the temple's destruction and its substitution by Jesus' risen body, the Church.

So in trying to determine what actually happened, critical scholarship generally concludes that, if Jesus cleansed the temple at all, he did so in the expectation that it would indeed continue, and that he was simply performing a reforming act that was well within the prophetic tradition. It is generally held to be less likely that he predicted the temple's destruction (though even in the 30s AD, given the unstable political situation in Israel, it must always have been on the cards). But it is generally thought unlikely that he foretold his own resurrection and the identification of his risen body with a church. The most common scholarly view is that these sayings have been read back into the story by the evangelist, writing after, or near to, the destruction of the temple by the Romans in 70 AD, who naturally understood the destruction as God's punishment on Israel for rejecting their Messiah, and saw the Church as being now the new or true Israel, to whom the promises made to the old Israel had now passed.

On similar grounds most would question the historicity of the story of the fig tree. Quite apart from modern doubts about its 'miraculous' element, or the other objections to its 'morality' which we have mentioned, the central *meaning* of the story is most unlikely to derive from Jesus himself – and it is the central meaning of the story that is, and ought to be perceived as, the most objectionable. The point of the story is that God has now finally visited his people Israel, that they have failed to bear the fruit that was expected of them, and that therefore from now on they are cursed and doomed to die: 'May no one ever eat fruit from you again';

'what I gave them has passed from them'. How likely is it that Jesus abrogated God's promise and cursed his own nation, in word or in deed? The idea that Israel was cursed for rejecting Jesus is not a leading theme in Mark, but it is undeniably present here, as in the parable of the vineyard and the tenants. It is still more explicit in the later Gospels of Matthew and John. It is an idea that is impossible to ascribe to Jesus himself, but which, having arisen as a result of the events of 70 AD, was then further reinforced in 85 AD when Christians were formally expelled from the Jewish synagogues. It stands in sharp contrast to the view of Paul, writing before 70 AD, who despite his own rejection by his fellow Jews was always clear that Israel remains God's people and that God's election and promise remain irrevocable. Using an image that is almost the reverse of the fig tree, Paul insists that the Jews remain, as they always were, God's original planting; and maintains the hope that one day both Gentile Christians and Jews will again be 'grafted' together to form a single, living tree.[8]

Meaning for Today

Many people, reading the story of the fig tree at a superficial level, have found it nasty for the wrong reason, because it seems to give Jesus an unreasonably petulant and irritable character. Having looked at the tradition and meaning behind the story a little more deeply, we have uncovered a right reason for finding it even nastier. It exemplifies the way the early Church imported into the Gospel an anti-Semitic ideology which had no place in the original teaching of Jesus, and which has spawned a terrible legacy of atrocities perpetrated by Christians on Jews down the ages.

Perceiving the extent to which this anti-Jewish theology

pervades the New Testament writings, especially those of the period after the events of 70 and 85 AD, has been a major feature of New Testament scholarship in recent years, and it is important that Christians take it on board. To do so is not to deny the uniqueness of Jesus as the Jewish Messiah, nor to underplay his sharp criticisms of the Judaism of his day, nor to pretend that the Christian and Jewish faiths are closer than they are. Rather, it is to try to counteract a prejudice that was embedded in the Christian tradition from near its beginning. It arose from three factors: first, the misinterpretation of the temple's destruction by the Romans in 70 AD as God's punishment of the Jews for the death of Jesus; secondly, resentment against the Jewish edict of 85 AD which condemned Christians as heretics and put them out of the synagogue; and thirdly, the motive, which emerges especially in the passion narratives, to make the Christian faith acceptable to the Roman state by shifting the blame for Jesus' death so far as possible from the Roman authorities, and laying it on the Jews. All these factors have conditioned the Gospel stories and disfigured their presentation of Jesus and his teaching in varying degrees. That fact may be awkward for Christians who cling to the notion of biblical 'inerrancy', but recognizing it is necessary if we genuinely wish to heal and counteract its grim legacy of Christian anti-Semitism.

Above all, the notion that God has cursed the Jews for the death of Jesus – so vividly encapsulated in the blasting of the fig tree, or in the Jews' chorus in Matthew's passion narrative ('His blood be on us and on our children' [27:25], a notion that is still current in benighted parts of the Christian Church and used to justify hatred of Jews) – must be rooted out of Christian teaching and Christian consciousness. Recognizing that the New Testament speaks with more than one voice on this issue, we need to align ourselves consciously with Paul and against the evangelists, in particular, with Paul's continuing love and respect for the tradition of Israel, his unbreakable conviction that God's promises stand firm, and his yearning hope that in the end all Israel – the Old and the New – shall be one in God's salvation.

We might also be justified in seeing a second level of meaning in the fig tree for today, provided we are willing to see in it a curse and condemnation of ourselves, and not of others. Jesus was certainly in anguish over the fruitlessness, corruption and spiritual blindness of the religious institutions of his time. Is he likely to be in any less anguish over ours? Will he find more of the fruits of righteousness in ours? His prophetic action in cleansing the court of the Gentiles strongly suggests that he shared the perception of Zechariah and Isaiah, that the self-serving, self-preoccupied worldliness of the religious establishment repelled people, and prevented the temple realizing its prophesied destiny of becoming a 'house of prayer for all nations'. Is it likely that he thinks much differently of his Church now? It is always worth asking ourselves Malachi's question, 'What would the Lord do now if he suddenly appeared in the midst?' How much of our religion will be thrown down as self-seeking, trivial, hypocritical, mechanical and meaningless when the time of judgement comes and the whirlwind begins to turn? How far does our Church, with its grand boast to be the Body of Christ on earth, actually exemplify Christ's life of radical service, his sacrificial love, his freedom from the world and its fake securities, his uncompromising truth-telling, his unconditional acceptance and inclusion of the most poor and despised, his willingness to live by the mystery of losing yourself to find your true self? And since that Church is nothing but we ourselves – since we ourselves are the limbs of this body, the branches of this vine, the members of this New Israel, the living stones of this new Temple – how much of our miserable failure is down to me?

For Prayer and Meditation

You brought a vine out of Egypt: you drove out the nations and planted it in.

You cleared the ground before it: and it struck root and filled the land.

The hills were covered with its shadow: and its boughs were like the boughs of the great cedars.

It stretched out its branches to the sea: and its tender shoots to the Great River.

Why then have you broken down its walls: so that every passer-by can pluck its fruit?

The wild boar out of the woods roots it up: and the locusts from the wild places devour it.

Turn to us again O Lord of hosts: look down from heaven and see.

Bestow your care upon this vine: the stock which your own right hand has planted.

Let your power rest on the man at your right hand: on that son of man whom you made so strong for yourself.

And so shall we not turn back from you; give us life and we will call upon your name.

Restore us again O Lord of hosts: show us the light of your countenance and we shall be saved.

Psalm 80:8–15,17–19

Be on your guard against the Jews, knowing that wher-
ever they have their synagogues, nothing is found but a
den of devils. They are nothing but thieves and robbers
who daily eat no morsel and wear no thread of clothing
which they have not stolen and pilfered from us by their
accursed usury. I shall give you my sincere advice. First,
to set fire to their synagogues and schools and to bury
and cover with dirt whatever will not burn, so that no
one will ever again see a stone or cinder of them. This is
to be done to the honour of our Lord and of Christen-
dom. Second, I advise that their houses be razed and
destroyed. Instead they might be lodged under a roof or
barn, like the gypsies. This will bring home to them that
they are not masters in our country, but living in exile
and captivity. Third, I advise that all their prayer books
and Talmudic writings, in which such idolatry, lies, cursing and blasphemy are taught, be taken from them.
Fourth, I advise that their rabbis be forbidden to teach
henceforth on pain of loss of life or limb. Fifth, I advise
that safe conduct on the highways be completely abol-
ished for Jews. Sixth, I advise that usury be prohibited to
them, and that all cash and treasure of silver and gold be
taken from them and put aside for safekeeping. Seventh,
I commend putting a flail, an axe, a hoe, a distaff or a
spindle into the hands of young, strong Jews and
Jewesses, and letting them earn their bread in the sweat
of their brow, as was imposed on the children of Adam.
If this does not help, we must drive them out like mad
dogs, so that we do not become partakers of their abominable blasphemy and all their other lies, and thus merit
God's wrath and be damned with them. I have done my
duty. Now let everyone see to his. I am exonerated.

Martin Luther[9]

O God, we are conscious that many centuries of blindness have blinded our eyes so that we no longer see the beauty of thy chosen people, nor recognize in their faces the features of our privileged brethren. We realize that the mark of Cain stands upon our foreheads. Across the centuries our brother Abel has lain in the blood which we drew or which we caused to be shed by forgetting thy love. Forgive us for the curse we falsely attached to their name as Jews. Forgive us for crucifying thee a second time in their flesh. For we knew not what we did.

Pope John XXIII

Lord, do something about your Church.
It is so awful, it is hard not to feel ashamed of belonging
    to it.
Most of the time it seems to be all the things you
    condemned:
hierarchical, conventional, judgmental, hypocritical,
respectable, comfortable, moralising, compromising,
clinging to its privileges and worldly securities,
and when not positively objectionable, merely absurd.
Lord we need your whip of cords.
Judge us and cleanse us,
challenge and change us,
break and remake us.
Help us to be what you called us to be.
Help us to embody you on earth.
Help us to make you real down here,
and to feed your people bread instead of stones.
And start with me.

Jeffrey John

There is hope for a tree,
even if it be cut down, that it will sprout again,
and that its shoots will not cease.
Though its root grow old in the earth,
and its stump die in the ground,
yet at the scent of water it will bud
and put forth branches like a young plant.

Job 14:7

17

The Crippled Woman

Now Jesus was teaching in one of the synagogues on the Sabbath. And just then there appeared a woman with a spirit that had crippled her for eighteen years. She was bent over and was quite unable to stand up straight. When Jesus saw her, he called her over and said, 'Woman, you are set free from your ailment'. When he laid his hands on her, immediately she stood up straight and began praising God. But the leader of the synagogue, indignant because Jesus had cured on the Sabbath, kept saying to the crowd, 'There are six days on which work ought to be done; come on those days and be cured, and not on the sabbath day'. But the Lord answered him and said, 'You hypocrites! Does not each of you on the sabbath untie his ox or his donkey from the manger, and lead it away to give water? And ought not this woman, a daughter of Abraham whom Satan bound for eighteen long years, be set free from this bondage on the sabbath day?' When he said this, all his opponents were put to shame; and the entire crowd was rejoicing at all the wonderful things he was doing.

Luke 13:10–17

Commentary

This story appears only in Luke. At first sight the focus seems to be on the fact that Jesus healed on the Sabbath. In this it resembles the story of Jesus healing the man with the withered hand,[1] as well as John's stories of the healing of the blind man, and of the crippled man at Beth-Zatha. It is particularly close to the short story of the healing on a Sabbath of the man with dropsy, also found only in Luke,[2] with which it is perhaps intended to form a pair. In all these stories of Sabbath healing the fact that Israel's leaders are unable to rejoice in the manifest good that Jesus does, but through jealousy prefer to denigrate him as a lawbreaker, demonstrates not only their pettiness but their fundamental blindness and blasphemy. It is an instance of the 'sin against the Spirit',[3] which consists precisely in calling evil good and good evil, and which aligns the Pharisees with the warped powers that finally bring Jesus to the cross. This reversal of basic values on their part is compounded by their personal hypocrisy: they will do the work of untying and watering their own animals on the Sabbath[4] or of rescuing them from a pit,[5] but they will condemn Jesus for supposedly breaking the Sabbath by rescuing his fellow human beings from bondage to sickness and death. They have forgotten the original meaning and purpose of the Sabbath – to bring people release and freedom, not further burdens of oppression – and in doing so they have become instruments of oppression themselves.

The element of Sabbath controversy in this story should not, however, make us overlook the wider and deeper meaning of the healing. The crippled woman is said to have been literally 'bowed down' by eighteen years of oppression by a 'spirit of infirmity', apparently a spinal ailment, which is directly attributed to Satan's power. Like so many of the objects of Jesus' healing – lepers, Samaritans, tax-collectors, the paralysed, the 'unclean' in general – she represents a category of those who lived on the margins, who were at least partially excluded from society, and cut off from freedom and the fullness of life. The healing that Jesus effects here, as in all the miracles, symbolizes far more than the healing of an individual or of an individual disease: rather, it proclaims the overcoming of all the forces of sickness and oppression, and the joyful inclusion of those whom they had formerly excluded. By far the most important point of this miracle is the same as that of the healing of the woman with a haemorrhage: Jesus is determined to subvert the power of the taboos and prejudices which subjugated and 'crippled' women in his own society.

A number of features in the story pinpoint different aspects of this act of social and religious liberation. First, it is significant that the woman is called out by Jesus from the margins of the synagogue and made to stand in the middle – as if to demonstrate that she was of equal standing with the men who alone could claim a right to be there. Next, Jesus lays his hands on her – overturning, as in several other cases we have seen, both the rules of social propriety and the levitical rules which forbade a man, and especially a rabbi, from risking possible contamination from menstrual impurity. Jesus then addresses her as a 'daughter of Abraham' – a title which seems to be peculiar to Luke, but which again clearly implies her equality with the 'sons of Abraham', as a full member of God's people. Finally, and most marvellously, she is able to *stand up and hold her head high* – just as Jesus in Luke tells the disciples they are to 'stand up and hold their heads high' when the time of their redemption is near.[6] Unburdened from the weight of cultural and spiritual oppression, from now on the woman is to play her part as an equal member, with equal dignity, in the new social and religious order inaugurated by Jesus.

It is worth observing that a number of other passages unique to Luke confirm that, of all the evangelists, he was most determined to record and substantiate this startlingly new and liberating attitude to women on Jesus' part. Women play a specially prominent role in his Gospel. It is Luke who gives us Mary in his birth and infancy narrative as the embodiment of all that was best in faithful Israel's past: the representative of Israel's faithful, humble poor vindicated by God; the literal Daughter of Zion that the Prophets foretold would bring forth the saviour; the ultimate Ark or Temple of the Covenant, 'overshadowed' and indwelt by the Spirit to be the vessel of God's very presence in the world'; the obedient servant whose 'Yes' made possible the incarnation, and ensured that all generations call her blessed. It is Luke who gives us Elizabeth, the Baptist's mother, whose own immediate faith and recognition of God's work in Mary is contrasted with the questioning doubt of her priestly husband Zechariah. It is Luke who gives us the story of Mary and Martha, with its unavoidable implication that the best place for women is not in the kitchen but doing theology! It is Luke who gives us the importunate widow, holding her up as a model of constant prayer, nagging and battering the ears of the Judge until he bestirs himself to do something (it is worth noting that like the Syrophoenician or Canaanite woman,[7] or like John's Samaritan woman,[8] she is commended precisely for *not* being submissive, but rather for challenging the legal and religious status quo for women, and asserting her right to be heard). Finally it is Luke who, uniquely in the New

Testament, portrays God in the person of a woman, in the parable of the housewife and the lost coin.

Walter Wink has summarized the meaning of Luke's miracle of crippled woman in a way that sums up the revolutionary implications of Jesus' dealings with women in general:

> By healing her on the Sabbath, Jesus restored the Sabbath to its original meaning of healing from bondage. By touching her, Jesus revoked the Holiness Code with its male scruples about menstrual uncleanness and sexual enticement. By speaking to her in public, Jesus jettisoned male restraints on the freedoms of women, born of the fear of female sexuality. By placing her in the middle of the synagogue, Jesus challenged the male monopoly on the means of grace and access to God. By asserting that her illness was not divine punishment for sin but satanic oppression, Jesus liberated her from domination, whose driving spirit is Satan. This tiny drama takes on world-historic proportions. In freeing this woman from Satan's power Jesus simultaneously released her from the encompassing network of patriarchy, male religious elitism, and the taboos fashioned to disadvantage some in order to preserve the advantage of others. Her physical ailment was symbolic of a system that literally bent women over. For her to stand erect in male religious space represents far more than a healing. It reveals the dawn of a whole new world order.[9]

Meaning for Today

The Church did not develop or perpetuate the liberating attitude that characterizes Jesus' treatment of women in the Gospels. The older, deep-rooted, negative attitudes to women gradually reasserted themselves, although the memory of Jesus' radically new approach could not completely be lost. There are clear signs of this reversion in the Pauline letters. In Galatians, an early epistle, Paul had boldly stated as a fundamental principle the new equality of all human beings in Christ: 'There is neither Jew nor Greek, there is neither slave nor free, there is neither male nor female; for you are all one in Christ Jesus'.[10] This famous verse encapsulates the theoretical ideal that derived from Jesus' own policy of radically inclusive equality. But it is questionable to what degree this policy was ever reflected in the real life of the Church. Even Jesus himself, despite the challenge that his own behaviour posed to conventional prejudice, still chose only men to be apostles – one must assume because it could not feasibly have been otherwise. To an even greater degree Paul clearly allowed his egalitarian Christian theory to be tempered by practical circumstances. In 1 Corinthians he offers some strikingly new teachings about female equality (especially in his teaching on the mutual rights and obligations of husbands and wives in chapter 7), but these are offset by a much more equivocal acceptance of women's participation in worship, provided they are veiled and acknowledge their subordination to men;[11] and finally by a blunt reassertion of the old attitudes in his command to women to keep silent in church and 'if there is anything they desire to know, to learn from their husbands at home'.[12] The post-Pauline letters complete this reversion and display an attitude to women that parallels that of the synagogue, bringing back even the doctrine that women, not men, are ultimately responsible for the Fall.[13]

Today the Church is still only beginning to make Jesus' inclusion of women and the egalitarian theory of Galatians

3:38 a visible reality in its life. The old prejudices and taboos that reasserted themselves after Jesus' time solidified in the patristic period (see the quotation from Tertullian below), and in most parts of the Church are still very much in place, even in societies where secular trends are more progressive. In many Western countries the Church, to its shame, is the only place in which the equal status of women, now taken for granted in the rest of society, may still be denied.

Galatians 3:28 pointed to the removal of the distinctions of race (Jew and Greek) and class (slave and free) as well as the distinction of sex, and it has often been observed that it also took a long time for the first two to be put into practice. The book of Acts, and Paul himself in Galatians 2, describe part of the struggle to include Gentiles within the Church on an equal footing with Jews, and the struggle continued well beyond the period of the New Testament – there were still Jewish-Christian sects that excluded Gentile membership in the third century. The equalization of 'slave and free' took much longer still. Despite the theoretical equality of slaves and masters 'in Christ', the practice of slavery continued to be countenanced by Paul himself and by the early Church.[14] Not until the eighteenth century did the Church begin to see that the notion of slavery itself is fundamentally incompatible with Jesus' teaching and attitudes. And when Christian prophets such as Wilberforce began to point this out, it is worth remembering that his most vehement opponents were 'traditionalist' and 'biblical' Christians – above all the Anglican bishops in the House of Lords! They could point out, quite correctly, that tradition, and Scripture itself, had always countenanced slavery. It was much harder to argue, as Wilberforce had to, that although the institution of slavery is literally accepted

in Scripture, nevertheless it stands against the essence of
Scripture and against the whole tenor of Christ's character
and attitudes, and should be overturned.

It is important to see the parallels between this
eighteenth-century argument about slavery, and our argument today about the equal inclusion of women in the life
of the Church. The same applies to the argument about gay
people and relationships. Nowadays few Christians would
doubt that the Holy Spirit was moving Wilberforce, while it
was largely a spirit of prejudice and self-interest that
was moving the Bishops. Yet for a long time Scripture and
tradition were taken to be on the Bishops' side, not
Wilberforce's – and their arguments were allowed to delay
the act of emancipation for many years. We may well judge
now, with hindsight, that Wilberforce and the emancipa-
tors were the ones who genuinely obeyed the *spirit* of
Scripture – but they only did so by refusing to be bound by
its *letter*, thus incurring the charge that they were 'unscriptural'. The same charge of disobeying Scripture was, of
course, the charge of the Scribes who opposed Jesus' healing
the crippled woman. It is always the charge of those who
stifle the living Word with the written word in order to
defend their prejudices and the status quo. And the living
Word may be stifled for a long time, but will prevail –
whether it takes three centuries to include Gentiles, or
eighteen to include slaves, or twenty-one to include women.

For Prayer and Meditation

No woman who has come to know the Lord and learned
the truth about her own (that is, the female) condition
would wish to adopt too cheerful (still less ostentatious)
a mode of dress. Rather she would go about in humble

clothing, with a downcast air, walking like Eve in mourning and penitence. Her dress should seek to atone for, to expiate what she inherits from Eve – namely the shame of the first sin, and the odium of being the cause of human downfall. 'In pain and distress you shall bear children; your desire shall be for your husband, and he shall rule over you'. Do you not know that each of you is an Eve? God's sentence on your sex continues to this day, and your guilt necessarily continues also. You are the devil's gateway. You are the one who unsealed the forbidden tree. You are the first to have broken the divine law. You are the one who persuaded the man, whom the devil was not brave enough to attack. You so easily destroyed God's image in man! It is on account of the punishment you deserved – death – that the Son of God himself had to die.

Tertullian, On the Apparel of Women 1

As regards the individual nature, woman is defective and misbegotten, for the active force in the male seed tends to the production of a perfect likeness in the masculine sex; while the production of a woman comes from a defect in the active force or from some material indisposition . . . It is unchangeable that a woman is destined to live under man's influence and has no authority from her Lord.

Thomas Aquinas, Summa Theologica 1.92

The Jesus movement began to glimpse the possibility of transforming the relationships of race (ethnicity), slavery, and sexism. . . . Paul anticipated this in the new relations of the baptized in the messianic community, where Jew and Greek, male and female, slaves and free would become brothers and sisters and work together in preaching and teaching. . . . However the egalitarian vision was not preserved as the normative tradition in the New Testament. The ambiguity of Paul towards this vision, and the patriarchalization of Christianity that occurred in the deuteropauline tradition, suppressed the early vision. Thus the countercultural egalitarian vision must be read between the lines in the New Testament. It must be ferreted out, in fragmentary form, in contrast to the patriarchal church which established the canonical framework for interpreting Christianity . . . In the New Testament a suppressed tradition must be brought to the surface . . .

Rosemary Radford Ruether[15]

What is the kingdom of God like? It's like more and more Bent-Over Women standing up. How can we know if the kingdom of God is actually coming? Why not look around and see if there are any formerly Bent-Over Women standing up? . . . Brother, if you ever see a Bent-Over Woman beginning to unbend and straighten herself, at the very least you had better give her a little standing room, because that isn't just another Bent-Over Woman standing up. That's *your sister* rising to her full stature – and that's *God's kingdom* cranking up! And sister, if for whatever reason you are still bent over and weighed down, and you think that's the way it was intended to be or must always be, then know that you have been given divine permission to straighten yourself fully and to stand up. And know too that since it is Satan who wants you to be a slave, only the Devil himself would say that *now* is not the time or *this* is not the place.

If your spirit is bent over, you are free to rise up! Let it be
so, brothers and sisters! Again and again and again, let it
be so!

YWCA Bible Study[16]

Bent over a fist full of twigs
twice daily, sweeping.
Bent beneath a load of wood or care.
Keeping the rules that keep
a woman bent by burdens,
spent with weeping.
A woman is bent.
Surely you meant
when you lifted her up
long ago to Your praise,
Compassionate One,
not one woman only,
but all women bent
by unbending ways.

Miriam Therese Winter[17]

God of the outsider
who in your servant Ruth
established the line of our salvation;
give us her love and courage
with all the women who wait
like strangers in your church,
to travel a new path;
put our faith in the faith of a woman,
and boldly claim your promise,
through Jesus Christ. Amen.

The St Hilda Community[18]

18

Two Resurrections

1. The Raising of the Widow's Son at Nain

Soon afterwards Jesus went to a town called Nain, and his disciples and a large crowd went with him. As he approached the gate of the town, a man who had died was being carried out. He was his mother's only son, and she was a widow; and with her was a large crowd from the town. When the Lord saw her, he had compassion on her and said to her, 'Do not weep'. Then he came forward and touched the bier, and the bearers stood still. And he said, 'Young man, I say to you, rise!' The dead man sat up and began to speak, and Jesus gave him to his mother. Fear seized all of them; and they glorified God, saying, 'A great prophet has risen among us!' and 'God has looked favourably on his people!' This word about him spread throughout Judea and all the surrounding country.

Luke 7:11–17

Commentary

The raising of the widow's son is a story peculiar to Luke's Gospel. The nearest Synoptic equivalent to it is the raising of Jairus's daughter, but in that case the child had very recently died, and was declared by Jesus to be 'only sleeping'. Here Jesus intercepts the funeral procession, and there is no possible doubt about the fact of death. The story, like that of Jairus's daughter, is a prefiguring of the resurrection of Jesus at the end of the Gospel; but a particular motive for including it at this point may be that, immediately following it, Jesus sends messengers to John the Baptist reporting that 'the blind are receiving their sight, the lame walk, lepers are cleansed, the deaf hear, the dead are raised' (Luke 7:22). Since the story of Jairus's daughter will not appear until much later in the Gospel, following the sequence Luke has borrowed from Mark, Luke may have wished to give some evidence of the dead being raised at this point, before the messengers were sent.

Luke's story is modelled on the raising of the widow's son at Zarephath, performed by Elijah in 1 Kings 17:8–34. In both stories the recently bereaved widow is met at the gate; in both the son of the widow is resuscitated; in both the miracle is acclaimed as testimony to the great godliness of the prophet (it is significant that the townspeople acclaim Jesus as 'a great *prophet*' in Luke's story); and finally, the phrase 'gave him to his mother' is identical to the Greek version of the Elijah story. Some commentators also find parallels with Hellenistic healing miracle stories, especially one about Apollonius of Tyana raising a dead girl, which describes the healer making the bearers stand still, touching the girl, and bringing her to life. This story, however, may post-date Luke. It is more likely that these details were part of the genre than that Apollonius was specifically in mind.

There is no doubt, however, about the direct influence of Elijah. Elijah was important to Luke. In Jewish tradition, following the prophecy in Malachi 4:5, Elijah was (and still is) supposed to return to usher in the messianic period. Matthew and Mark both identified him with John the Baptist. Luke, however, almost completely drops the link between Elijah and the Baptist, and instead shows Jesus himself fulfilling Elijah's role. Several stories about Jesus that occur only in Luke directly recall stories about Elijah: for example, the disciples' desire to call down fire on their enemies;[1] and the story of the disciple who wished to say goodbye to his family.[2] Only in Luke's Gospel does Jesus at the start of his ministry deliberately compare himself to Elijah and Elisha, both of whom had had a ministry to Gentiles; he specifically recalls the raising of the widow's son at Zarephath.[3] But as well as being attracted by Elijah as a forerunner of the Gentile mission, Luke was clearly strongly influenced as well by the tradition that having been taken up into heaven, Elijah sent down his spirit on Elisha, who continued his work and repeated some of his miracles. In the same way, it is only in Luke–Acts that Jesus ascends, and then sends down his Spirit upon the disciples, who are thus empowered to do works similar to his own. It is quite possible that this idea, and Luke's basic plan of writing Luke–Acts as a two-volume work around the fulcrum of Jesus' ascension, was inspired by the similar pattern of 1 and 2 Kings, which are separated by the story of Elijah's ascension.

There are, however, significant differences between the raising of the widow's son at Nain and the Elijah story: Jesus raises the man by the power of his word alone, whereas Elijah cried aloud to the Lord, begging him to heal the boy, and had to stretch himself over the boy three times. Luke's story makes it clear that the power to raise the dead lies in Jesus' own person. Neither is there any mention of a request for the miracle on the woman's part, nor is it a response to faith. It is an act of sheer grace occasioned by Jesus' compassion for her. So Luke identifies Jesus as Elijah's fulfilment, and is happy to have the townspeople of Nain hail him as a prophet; but at the same time he is clear that something greater than a prophet is here.

2. The Raising of Lazarus

Then Jesus, again greatly disturbed, came to the tomb. It was a cave, and the stone was lying against it. Jesus said, 'Take away the stone'. Martha, the sister of the dead man, said to him, 'Lord, already there has been a stench because he has been dead four days'. Jesus said to her, 'Did I not tell you that if you believed, you would see the glory of God?' So they took away the stone. And Jesus looked upward and said, 'Father, I thank you for having heard me. I knew that you always hear me, but I have said this for the sake of the crowd standing here, so that they may believe that you sent me'. When he had said this, he cried with a loud voice, 'Lazarus, come out!' The dead man came out, his hands and feet bound with strips of cloth, and his face wrapped in a cloth. Jesus said to them, 'Unbind him, and let him go'.

John 11:38-44

Commentary

The story of Lazarus is crucial to the dramatic structure of John's Gospel. It is placed at the midpoint of the story, the seventh sign of the so-called 'book of signs' that forms its first half. It is given as the single main cause of the plot against Jesus; it is central to the surrounding dialogue and discussion on the theme of resurrection; and it anticipates the resurrection of Jesus at the end.

Lazarus is a form of the Hebrew name Eleazar which means 'God helps'. Mary and Martha and Lazarus appear elsewhere only in Luke's Gospel,[4] with characters that correspond to John's portrayal of them, but there is no mention in Luke of Lazarus being their brother. In Luke Lazarus is a fictional figure, the poor man in the parable of the rich man and the beggar at his gate.[5] At the end of that parable Lazarus dies and goes 'to Abraham's bosom' in heaven. The rich man also dies and is sent to hell. In his torment he begs Abraham to send Lazarus back to earth, to warn his brothers, lest they too come to the place of torment. The punchline of Luke's parable is in Abraham's reply: 'I tell you, they will not believe even if one should rise from the dead'. It is hard to avoid the conclusion that John's Gospel, with its typically dark irony, has made Lazarus a real person, and made Luke's punchline come true. Lazarus does indeed come back from the dead; but so far from this causing others to believe, it becomes the main reason why Jesus himself is put to death.

Just as Luke's story of the widow's son 'improved' the story of Jairus's daughter by portraying the raising of one who was indisputably dead, John goes a step further by having Lazarus four days in the tomb – longer even than Jesus himself – and already beginning to decay. It may be relevant that there was an opinion among the rabbis that the soul hovered near the body three days, but that after that there was no hope of resuscitation. Jesus is here accomplishing the utterly impossible, to bring his friends back to life.

The story is remarkable for its depiction of Jesus'

extreme emotion. We have already been told[6] that Jesus wept for Lazarus, so that the bystanders said, 'see how much he loved him!' Before the tomb Jesus is said to 'shudder', and to be moved with the deepest emotion. Twice the same extraordinary word is used that Mark used in the story of Jesus healing the leper, a word that conveys the idea of flared nostrils – 'snorting with fury'. Here, too, it seems to imply deep anger as well as grief, not anger at the afflicted, but at the powers of evil that cause sickness, death and grief. Another rare and powerful Greek word is used to express Jesus' 'crying with a loud voice'. It is used again in this Gospel for the shout of the people for Barabbas in the passion story, and there may well be a deliberate contrast between Jesus' shout that hauls forth Lazarus into life, and the baying of the crowd that drives Jesus to his death.

The raising of Lazarus is a sort of double symbol, anticipating the resurrection both of Jesus and of the believer. Like Jesus' tomb, Lazarus's is sealed with a stone. Like Jesus he has been bound with strips of linen cloth and anointed with oils and spice. Like the cloth that wrapped Jesus' head,[7] the cloth that wrapped Lazarus's head is mentioned separately. By contrast, however, Lazarus comes forth bound to show that he has risen by another's power and will die again; whereas Jesus leaves his grave clothes behind because he rises by his own power, and will have no more need of them. At the same time the miracle is a sign for believers of the hope of their own resurrection. This is made clear at the start, when Lazarus's sickness and death are said to be 'to the glory of God'.[8] Jesus' strange-seeming prayer before the tomb makes the same point. In a sense, Jesus' prayer to the Father is unnecessary, because Jesus and the Father are one, and their will is one. Jesus therefore knows that his prayer is always heard. The prayer is for the benefit of the bystanders, not in the sense that 'Jesus is playing to the gallery', but so that they will understand a miraculous work that is done in the Father's power, and find faith and life through it.

The whole miracle story is worth comparing with the promise of Jesus in John 5:25–29 about the believer's judgement and eternal life. Notice the correspondence between the highlighted phrases and the Lazarus story.

> Very truly I tell you, the hour is coming, *and is now here, when the dead will hear the voice of the Son of God, and those who hear will live.* For just as the Father has life in himself, so he has granted the Son also to have life in himself; and *he has given him authority* to execute judgment, because he is the Son of Man. Do not be astonished at this; for the hour is coming when *all who are in their graves will hear his voice and will come out* – those who have done good to the *resurrection of life,* and those who have done evil, to the *resurrection of condemnation.*

The story of Lazarus dramatizes in detail the fulfilment of exactly that promise. In the context of this story, at least, Lazarus is 'the beloved disciple'. As R. L. Brown notes, 'Lazarus, the one whom Jesus loves, is . . . the representative of all those whom Jesus loves, namely the Christians. Just as Jesus gives life to his beloved Lazarus, so he will give life to his beloved Christians'.[9] Lazarus, in other words, stands for us.

Meaning for Today

Both Lazarus and the widow's son at Nain, like Jairus's daughter, rise from the dead to die again. Theirs is a temporary victory: they are resuscitated back into normal human life, rather than resurrected in the true Christian sense of the word. To be resurrected in the proper sense means to be no longer constrained by death or the limitations of the body. So whether or not we take the stories as being historically based, in either case they are still only pre-figurings of the resurrection that really matters – Jesus' and ours.

Jesus was resurrected in the fullest sense. Although the Gospels of Luke and John portray the resurrected Christ as still being able to share in physical embodiment for a limited period – perhaps for the sake of assuring the disciples that he is still truly alive, and that he is truly the same Jesus – nevertheless we understand that his resurrection and ours is to eternal life, and to a completely different mode of existence. As Paul expresses it, 'flesh and blood do not inherit the kingdom of God . . . but we shall be changed'.[10] However we may understand it, the resurrection 'body' or mode of existence is, Paul says, as unimaginably unlike this body as the seed is unlike the plant, or as the life of the foetus is unlike the life of the fully grown adult to be (1 Corinthians 15:35–50). But as the plant is continuous with the seed and the adult with the foetus, our new and eternal life will still be continuous with our old life. We will still be our real selves – in fact, much more our real selves when all the fake and nonsense are taken away – but uncon-strained by life in the body. That is not to say that the body is irrelevant, although it will certainly return to dust and ashes. We are psychosomatic creatures: the person I am is inseparably both soul and body. So it is an oversimpli-fication to think that at death our 'real' spiritual self 'escapes' from the body, as the Gnostics supposed. Rather, resurrection means that *everything* we are in this life, both body and soul, is redeemed by God and held by him. He will continue to hold it in being, just as he is the only source of its being now. And though the physical body is left behind, everything that it expressed and experienced in relation to our person is not. We shall not be less than we are in heaven, but infinitely more. That seems to be the truth that the resurrection appearances in Luke and John, which are much more 'physical' in character than those in Mark, Matthew and Paul, intend to convey.

It is important not to suppose that Christian faith in the resurrection depends on believing the literal and detailed historical truth of these miracle stories, nor even on the literal and detailed historical truth of the stories of Jesus' own resurrection. As we have seen throughout this study, the Gospel genre constantly mixes the historical with the interpretative and the symbolic, and it is often impossible to separate them out. It should be remembered, too, that our earliest witnesses, Paul and Mark, are silent about the physical mechanics of the resurrection and the nature of Jesus' resurrection body. But it is equally clear that in speaking of resurrection neither they nor any of the New Testament writers are speaking of a purely subjective vision on the part of the disciples, still less of resurrection as a psychological projection, or as a metaphor for this-worldly hopes or memories (as one might say 'Elvis lives', or 'Marx is still with us'). Paul, in the earliest account of all in 1 Corinthians 15, is writing in a soberly factual and historical genre, listing by name the eyewitnesses of an actual event – himself being the last of them. Whatever the mechanics of the resurrection, or the nature of Christ's risen life, he is clear that Christ conquered death and lives in the most real sense possible. Paul's evidence is all the more impressive because he was fully aware of the danger of his being misunderstood, and of being taken to be saying far less than he intended to say. The notion that the resurrection is no more than a metaphor for an inward spiritual experience, and nothing to do with personal survival beyond death, is not at all new. It was already around in Corinth, and has kept reappearing throughout the Church's history.[11] Paul is scathing about such sophistries, and flatly denies that those who hold them hold the Christian faith (1 Corinthians 15:17):

> If Christ has not been raised your faith is futile, . . . and those also who have died in Christ have perished. If it is for this life only that we have hoped in Christ, we are of all people most to be pitied.

Paul's conviction of the reality of resurrection led him to tell the Thessalonians 'not to grieve as those who have no hope'[12] – but he did not tell them not to grieve at all. Even when one knows it is temporary, separation from those we love most is still among the sharpest griefs for Christians, as for anyone else; and the prospect of our own death is hardly a less bitter one. The compassion of Jesus for the widow at Nain and his own extreme grief at Lazarus's death give the lie to those Christians who suggest that to grieve at all for a departed loved one shows lack of faith. True, part of Jesus' emotion at Lazarus's tomb expresses a kind of divine fury at the devastation that death and evil have wrought in creation; but his grief is portrayed as the grief of human bereavement too. Staring at his tears, the bystanders conclude, rightly, 'See how much he loved him!'[13] The New Testament is equally unashamed to portray Jesus' terror in the face of his own torture and death – in Gethsemane and on the cross he 'offered up prayers and supplications with loud cries and tears to the one who was able to save him'.[14] Jesus' capacity for grief and terror distinguish him from other classical heroes: the comparison has often been made with Socrates, facing death with philosophical calmness; and it seems to be very far from the British ideal of the 'stiff upper lip'. But for the author to the Hebrews, this capacity to suffer, and to enter into the sufferings of others, is part of what made Jesus truly human as well as divine, and therefore capable of being the Great High Priest who can relate us to God and God to us. It was for that reason that 'he had to be made like his brothers and sisters in every respect'.[15] Jesus' capacity to grieve honestly and openly for his friends and for himself might well make us wonder whether the stoical virtue of the stiff upper lip is really such a virtue at all. Christians, too, are called to be a royal priesthood, and we must know what passion is in order to be compassionate to others. When we lose someone who is worth more to us than life itself, or when the time comes for us to look our own death in the face, there is more comfort to be had in a friend who can grieve with us than in one who simply exhorts us to have faith and be brave; and there is infinitely more in a God who does the same.

For Prayer and Meditation

'Lazarus to Christ'

You are forgetting. I was indeed dead,
Not comatose, not sleeping, and could no more
Wish for resurrection than what we are before
Can wish for birth. I had already slid

Four days down when you hauled me back into the air.
Now they come to watch me break bread
And drink the wine, even the tactful plead
With dumb faces to be told something, and, dear,

Even you, who wept for me and of whom it is said
You know all things, what I mutter in nightmare
I believe you lie awake to overhear.
You too are curious, you too make me afraid

Of my own cold heart. However I wash,
I cannot get the foist out of my flesh.

'*Christ to Lazarus*'

They followed me when we came there, and I knew very
    well
They were already leaving me. Not one
Among your mourners had any stomach to go on,
And when we moved the stone and we could smell

Death in his lair they slid off me like a cloud
And left me shining cold on the open grave,
Crying for you and heaving until Death gave
And you were troubled in your mottled shroud.

They hid their eyes, they begged me let you stay,
But I was adamant, my friend. For soon
By a loving father fiercer than any moon
It will be done to me too, on the third day.

I hauled you out because I wanted to.
I never wept for anyone but you.

David Constantine[16]

Blessed are You,
O Tie That Binds
one person to another
in the miracle of love.
O Everlasting Moment,
O Hope That Never Dies,
be with the one
devastated
by death's visitation.
Be her life in death,
her hope in despair,
her promise of love everlasting,
now and for ever.
Amen.

Miriam Therese Winter[17]

You will not give me over to the power of death,
Nor suffer your faithful one to see the Pit.
You will show me the path of life; in your presence is
    the fullness of joy
And from your right hand flow delights for evermore.

Psalm 16:10,11

So death will come to fetch you? No, not death, but God
himself. Death is not the horrible spectre we see represented in pictures. The catechism teaches us that death is
the separation of the soul from the body; that is all. I am
not afraid of a separation that will unite me for ever with
God.

St Teresa of Avila

And thou, most kind and gentle death,
Waiting to hush our latest breath,
O praise him, alleluia!
Thou leadest home the child of God,
And Christ our Lord the way hath trod.
O praise him, O praise him,
Alleluia, alleluia, alleluia!

St Francis of Assisi

19

Two Miraculous Catches of Fish

1. The Miraculous Catch of Fish at the Calling of the Disciples

Once while Jesus was standing beside the lake of Gennesaret, and the crowd was pressing in on him to hear the word of God, he saw two boats there at the shore of the lake; the fishermen had gone out of them and were washing their nets. He got into one of the boats, the one belonging to Simon, and asked him to put out a little way from the shore. Then he sat down and taught the crowds from the boat. When he had finished speaking, he said to Simon, 'Put out into deep water and let down your nets for a catch'. Simon answered, 'Master, we have worked all night long and caught nothing. Yet if you say so, I will let down the nets'. When they had done this, they caught so many fish that their nets were beginning to break. So they signalled their partners in the other boat to come and help them. And they came and filled both boats, so that they began to sink. But when Simon Peter saw it, he fell down at Jesus' knees saying, 'Go away from me, Lord, for I am a sinful man!' For he and all who were with him were amazed at the catch of fish that they had taken; and so also were James and John, sons of Zebedee, who were partners with Simon. Then

Jesus said to Simon, 'Do not be afraid; from now on you will be catching people'. When they had brought their boats to shore, they left everything and followed him.

Luke 5:1–11

2. The Miraculous Catch of Fish after the Resurrection

Just after daybreak, Jesus stood on the beach, but the disciples did not know that it was Jesus. Jesus said to them, 'Children, you have no fish, have you?' They answered him, 'No'. He said to them, 'Cast the net to the right side of the boat, and you will find some'. So they cast it, and now they were not able to haul it in because there were so many fish. That disciple whom Jesus loved said to Peter, 'It is the Lord!' When Simon Peter heard that it was the Lord, he put on some clothes, for he was naked, and jumped into the sea. But the other disciples came in the boat, dragging the net full of fish, for they were not far from the land, only about a hundred yards off. When they had gone ashore, they saw a charcoal fire there, with fish on it, and bread. Jesus said to them, 'Bring some of the fish that you have just caught'. So Simon Peter went aboard and hauled the net ashore, full of large fish, a hundred and fifty-three of them; and although there were so many, the net was not torn.

John 21:4–11

Commentary

The story of the miraculous catch of fish appears only in Luke and John, but it is used by the two evangelists in two entirely different contexts. In Luke, it is attached to the story of the call of Peter, James and John (Andrew is not specifically mentioned), probably with the aim of amplifying the very bare account of the call of these first four disciples as it appears in Mark and Matthew. In John, the story forms the start of chapter 21, which has been bolted on rather clumsily to the text of the Gospel, apparently to satisfy the tradition of a resurrection appearance in Galilee, as recorded in Mark and Matthew. (The continuation of the story in John 21 has the further function of explicitly rehabilitating Peter – Jesus' triple command 'Feed my sheep . . . feed my lambs' corresponding to Peter's three denials of Jesus in the passion story [John 18:15–27].)

Which was the original setting of the story, or what experience underlies it, is now impossible to say. Some argue that the resurrection context is original because in Luke's story Peter calls Jesus 'Lord' (*Kyrie*) even before the miracle takes place, and because after it he falls at Jesus' feet confessing his sin, which fits best in a context after his betrayal of Jesus. Alternatively, some argue that the Lukan context is original because the disciples were far more likely to be found fishing before their call by Jesus, than to have returned to it after the resurrection. As the story stands in John's Gospel, it is extremely hard to explain why the disciples have returned to fishing after their stupendous experience of the resurrection and their commissioning by the risen Christ in chapter 20!

Whether the original context of the story was before or after the resurrection, and whatever lies behind it historically, its symbolic meaning is clearly tied to the words of Jesus at the call of the disciples in the Synoptics, 'I will make you fishers of people'. The miracle is a dramatic enactment, like the prophetic *oth* or 'acted word' of the mission of the apostles and the inclusion of people in the Church. Indeed, it may well be that the story itself was originally a parable, similar to, or even the same as, the parable of the dragnet and fish in Matthew 13:47–50, which later became dramatized into a miracle story. Still further back in the tradition, the image probably derives ultimately from Ezekiel's vision of the river of life flowing from the restored temple, where the catch of abundant fish is a sign of the ingathering of God's people in the last days:

> Wherever the river goes, every living creature that swarms will live, and there will be very many fish . . . People will stand fishing by the sea from En-Gedi to En-Eglaim; it will be a place for the spreading of nets; its fish will be of a great many kinds, like the fish of the Great Sea.[1]

There are examples of early Christian art depicting Peter and John holding a net either side of a stream flowing from the temple, which show that the Ezekiel reference behind it was not lost on the early Church.

In Luke's version the focus of the story is firmly on Peter. James and John are introduced late and rather awkwardly, almost as an afterthought, and Andrew is forgotten. Peter is very much the head and representative disciple here. His penitent reaction to Jesus must be understood as a reaction to this revelation of Jesus' authority, almost as to a theophany, rather than as an indication of some particular sin. It is a dominant theme in Luke that Jesus comes to call not the righteous but sinners to repentance; repentance must precede conversion, and so it is appropriate that repentance precedes the call of his first disciple. In John's story, although Peter remains pre-eminent and leaps in the sea to go to Jesus, it is the beloved disciple who first *recognizes* Jesus, rather as, in chapter 20, it is the beloved disciple who reaches the tomb first and sees it empty, but Peter who goes in. Although the authors of the two chapters are probably different, they evidently shared the same tradition about the two disciples' relative temperaments.

One or two oddities in the above translation of John 21 need explaining. Jesus calls the disciples 'children' but *paidia* can also mean 'lads', 'boys' or 'mates', as used in a group of adult friends. It also makes little sense that a naked Peter puts on clothes to go swimming. '*Gymnos*' can mean 'lightly clothed' as well as naked, and the verb translated as 'put on' actually means 'gird' or 'tuck in', so the sense is something like 'Peter tucked in the little clothing he was wearing . . .'

The symbolism of the story in John is more elaborated. In Luke, the fact that the nets were almost breaking is simply a sign of the size of the catch. In John, the emphasis on the fact that the net was *not* torn strongly suggests that the net stands for the Church, holding such a huge diversity of people in unity. The imagery and the meaning are the same as those of the seamless and untorn garment of Jesus in John's passion narrative – in both cases the verbs meaning 'tear' imply '*without schism*'. The number of fish – 153 – has given rise to many speculations down the centuries. Two in particular have gained wide acceptance. First, in rabbinic numerology 153 is a 'triangular number' on the base of 17; the numbers 17 and 3 both signify completion or perfection. The number therefore symbolizes the fullness or universality of the Church's mission. The second theory, which does not exclude the first, is that the number is connected by *gematria* (the calculation of the numerical value of Hebrew letters) with the names En-Gedi and En-Eglaim

– making it a hidden reference to the Ezekiel passage. Finally, there is a special significance too in the disciples' *hauling* the net ashore. The same verb is used at several points in the Gospel which speak of people being *drawn* to Jesus, and particularly in his prophecy, 'When I am lifted up I will draw all people to myself'.[2] In Johannine thinking the resurrection is part of the process of Jesus being 'lifted up' to the Father, taking humanity with him. In this story we see the risen Christ beginning to accomplish that prophecy of 'drawing all to himself' through the apostolic ministry, symbolized in the catch of fish and the hauling ashore.

Meaning for Today

Evangelism has long had a bad press. The very word has come to suggest for many people the stereotypical mass-evangelist who engineers conversions by intimidation and emotional manipulation, often for financial and always for egotistical gain. Much the same might be said of the word 'mission', which despite its wider meaning of social as well as verbal outreach is tainted by suggestions of colonialism and condescension, and carries with it the musty feel of the Victorian 'mission-hall'. In our time greater awareness of other religions has led to an increased embarrassment about the very concept of pushing one's own. In a plural society proselytizing becomes undesirable, even dangerous, and there is plenty of evidence in the world of the misery caused by religious differences and rivalries. The truth is, one can only ever say 'share my God, my beliefs, my ethics, my culture' from the conviction that these are in some way or to some degree superior to the other person's. So the very act of evangelism, however sensitively approached, may

easily be perceived as a judgement, a put-down or a
downright insult. It might also be said that the image of
'netting' and 'catching' people hardly helps. It suggests
entrapment – and what is the purpose of catching fish if not
to devour them? Many who were once converted by the
more manipulative kinds of evangelism have felt they were
trapped into a psychological straitjacket that repressed
their freedom and personality, and from which they later
found it extremely hard to free themselves – usually aban-
doning the Christian faith altogether.

Yet the command stands, 'Go make disciples of all
nations' (Matthew 28:19). Christians are still to be 'fishers
of people', but how to avoid so many negative, sometimes
repellent ways of doing it? Peter's reaction in Luke's story is
instructive. He has already seen something of Jesus; Jesus
has visited his house, and healed his mother-in-law. He has
already heard some of Jesus' teaching, though we do not
know what. But after the catch of fish – though not necessarily because of it – the penny drops. Something changes in
his perception, and he sees something of who and what
Jesus really *is*. It is a kind of theophany – a self-revelation of
God. Peter's reaction will be understood by most Christians
(one hopes all Christians) who have shared this experience
of suddenly feeling the reality of Jesus' presence: the sudden
collapse of the insides; the awareness not only of seeing
but of being seen, entirely; the welling of tears; the sense
of smallness, unworthiness, of needing to crawl beneath
the nearest stone, as if before a great, searching light. The
strangest thing is that simultaneously the most gut-
wrenchingly awful part *and* the most wonderful part of the
experience is realizing that one is loved *as one is*. Peter's
words, 'Depart from me, Lord, for I am a sinful man', are
the authentic response of someone feeling himself, unbear-

ably, exposed to the glare of this vast, unconditional love. He can't bear it, he wants to run and hide; yet having known it, he could never let it go. He will give up everything to follow it.

This is a conversion experience, but it does not only happen once, as Peter's own story tells. There was another time when the reality of himself was shown up against Christ's love, 'and he went out and wept bitterly'. Perhaps there was another after that, when again he tried to run away from the glory of his own painful destiny, but had to turn again and face it. In most Christian lives there are many conversions, as God shapes us into what he wants us to be. No doubt at some point there must be such a 'conversion experience' for every Christian. But to try to manufacture it in others is a terrible blasphemy. Only God's Spirit can do it, and the Spirit blows where it wills. Yes, we can prepare the ground – as Luke suggests Jesus did – by teaching, by service to others, by praying for them and simply being with them, though the thought of doing any of these things simply to get a new Christian 'scalp' is disgusting enough. Deliberately to manipulate the psychology and emotions of others is worse still – it is to usurp God's place and violate the human person, an adultery against God's love.

John's image of the victorious Christ 'drawing all people to himself' is a happier image for the Church's outreach than that of catching them in a net. It is an image of free attraction and inclusion rather than one of entrapment and coercion. It is also a reminder that mission is first the work of Christ himself; the Church can only ever be a partner in it, and only then insofar as its methods reflect his. The aspect of inclusion is especially important, and it is directly connected to the attraction. As we have seen, so many of the miracle stories themselves focus on Jesus' will to embrace and include all the categories of the excluded. To say the least, he sat light to the barriers that his own society raised against the marginalized. The Gospels present him as one of the most gloriously free, unprejudiced, uninhibited – and therefore attractive – individuals who ever walked the earth. The Churches are very far from modelling the same attitudes. That is partly because many parts of the Church prefer to dispense law, not grace. They have not grasped that conversion is a lifelong process; they expect it to be instantly completed at the start of the Christian life. Christian standards of morality (usually interpreted very narrowly as conventional respectability, and all too often only in terms of sex) are presented as entrance qualifications, rather than as goals to which all are aiming but may not yet have reached. The point of the parable of the drag-net in Matthew is that the Church has no business making this kind of judgement. The Church exists to include 'good' and 'bad' alike. Judgement will come later, and will be for God, not us – when we will no doubt find that his criteria are considerably different from ours. The Church is not a sanctuary for the perfected – or those who imagine themselves so to be. It is a free hospital for wounded and joyful sinners who are in the process of being healed. When it finds the humility to see itself that way, it will instantly become infinitely more attractive, as Christ was attractive – by drawing to him all those on the outside who feel 'unqualified' to come in.

For Prayer and Meditation

In the passage before us [John 21:4–11] Jesus shows by an outward action what the Church will be like at the end of the world. In the earlier passage about a catch of fish [Luke 5:1–11] he indicated the Church's present character. The fact that he performed the first at the start of his preaching, and this later miracle after his resurrection, shows that the first symbolises the good and bad presently co-existing in the Church, and the second symbolises only the good, who will be contained eternally, when the resurrection of the dead is completed at the end of the world. In the first miracle, Jesus stood not on the shore, but 'entered into one of the ships which was Simon's, and asked him to put out a little from the land'; in the second he remained on the shore. In the first miracle the fishes that were caught were put into the ship, and not, as in the second miracle, dragged to the shore. These and other clues show that on the first occasion the Church is prefigured as it exists in the world, and in the second as it shall be at the end of the world.

Augustine of Hippo, Homilies on the Gospel of John 122.7

Lord Jesus Christ, you stretched out your arms of love on the hard wood of the cross, that all might come within reach of your saving embrace. So clothe us in your spirit, that we reaching forth our hands in love, may bring those who do not know you to the knowledge and love of you, for your own love and mercy's sake.

American Episcopal Prayer Book

O guide me, call me, draw me,
uphold me to the end;
and then in heaven receive me,
my Saviour and my Friend.

J. E. Bode

All we can do is nothing worth unless God blesses the
    deed;
vainly we hope for the harvest-tide till God gives life to
    the seed.
Yet nearer and nearer draws the time, the time that shall
    surely be,
when the earth shall be filled with the glory of God as
    the waters cover the sea.

A. C. Ainger

Did you know that you can help fish for men with the
Internet, just by turning on your computer? If you make
'Fish The Net' your home page, each time you switch on
it sends out two Gospel banners to secular sites, each of
which can bring people to one of our cybertracts where
the Gospel is clearly presented . . .

Internet advertisement

It is this English Church, snug and smug among the
hedgerows, that has done it. That is the astonishing
thing. It has thrown feelers out so far and wide. It has
overleaped the paddock fence. It has flung out its frontier
line. It has set sail with every wind that blows, and
planted its feet on every shore that ocean washes. Who
would have dreamed it of her? She hardly believes it
herself. She finds it difficult to remember as she sits tied
up in Elizabethan red tape, and smothered under the
conventions of Establishment, and fat with dignities, and
very scant of breath. Yet it is all true. For here were the
adventurers whom she had sent out, trooping home to
din the story into her dim, deaf ears.

Henry Scott Holland[3]

Notes

1. *The Meaning of the Miracles*

1. Text adapted from my essay 'Making Sense of Scripture', in *Living Tradition*, ed. J. John, DLT, 1991, pp 44–45.
2. On the Gospel of John 24:2.
3. Deuteronomy 8:3.
4. Mark 1:22.
5. Luke 13:16.
6. Mark 4:39.
7. Isaiah 49:24–25; Luke 11:22.
8. Matthew 12:31; Mark 3:28–30.
9. Romans 13:1.
10. 1 Corinthians 2:8; Ephesians 6:12.
11. Colossians 1:16–20.
12. Matthew 12:28.
13. Matthew 11:21; Mark 8:17–21.
14. Matthew 11:2–5; cf. Isaiah 61:1; 35:5.
15. John 2:11,23.
16. John 7:3,4.
17. Mark 8:12; Matthew 12:38; Luke 11:28–30.
18. See G. Vermes, *Jesus the Jew*, Fontana, 1973, esp. chs. 1 and 3.
19. Matthew 12:27.
20. Mark 6:7,13; cf. 8:33.
21. John 6:26; 7:4–5.
22. John 10:38.
23. John 14:11.
24. Mark 8:17–18.
25. Mark 4:11–12.

26. Romans 11:25.
27. Isaiah 35:5.
28. John 14:12.

2. The Healing of a Leper

1. Leviticus 13:45.
2. Pilch, J., 'Healing in Mark: A Social Science Analysis', *Biblical Theology Bulletin* 15.4 (1985), pp 142,149.
3. Montefiore, H., *The Synoptic Gospels*, vol i, p 39.
4. Wink, Walter, *The Powers That Be*, Doubleday, 1998, p 75.
5. Myers, Ched, *Binding the Strong Man*, Orbis Books, 1998, p 146.
6. 'Outwitted', Edwin Markham, in *The Poems of Edwin Markham*, ed. C. L. Wallis, Harper Collins, 1959.
7. Julian of Norwich, *The Revelation of Divine Love*, ch.28

3. The Healing of the Paralysed Man

1. Matthew 9:2–8.
2. John 20:23.
3. Exodus 20:5; 34:7.
4. Smith, Martin L., *Reconciliation*, Mowbray, 1985, pp 7–8.
5. 'Confession', George MacDonald, in *George MacDonald: Poetical Works*, Johannesen Publishing, 1996.

4. The Wedding at Cana in Galilee

1. Matthew 25:1–12.
2. Matthew 22:1–10.
3. Matthew 22:11–14.
4. Luke 12:35–38.
5. Luke 14:7–11.
6. Revelation 19:7–9; 21:1–4.
7. Mark 2:19–22.
8. Amos 9:13–14; Hosea 14:7; Jeremiah 31:12; 1 Enoch 10:19.
9. 2 Baruch 29:5.
10. *Legum allegoriae* 3:82.
11. Mark 1:27.

12. Mark 3:21.
13. Luke 11:27.
14. Acts 2:13–15.
15. John Chrysostom, *Homilies on the Gospel of John*, 56.3.
16. Lang, Cosmo Gordon, *The Miracles of Jesus as the Way of Life*, Isbister & Sons, 1901, pp 35–6.

5. The Feeding of the Five Thousand and the Feeding of the Four Thousand

1. Numbers 27:17.
2. Ezekiel 34:11–16.
3. Isaiah 25:6–8.
4. Proverbs 9:1–5; Ecclesiasticus 15:3.
5. Mark 8:19–21.
6. Deuteronomy 8:3.
7. Hosea 11:5; 13:5,6.
8. *1 Enoch* 62:1–4.
9. Nineham, D. E., *Saint Mark*, Penguin, 1963, p 179.
10. John 6:52–58.

6. Two Sea-Miracles

1. Mark 1:25.
2. Rawlinson, E. R., *The Gospel According to St Mark*, Westminster Press, 1925, p 88.
3. Matthew 14:18–31.
4. Tertullian, *On Baptism* 12

7. The Gerasene Demoniac

1. *The Jewish War* 6:9:1.
2. Theissen, G., The Miracle Stories of the Early Christian Tradition, T. & T. Clark, 1983, p 256.
3. Mark 1:24.
4. See Bibliography.
5. See N. and G. Shiri, 'Dalits and Christianity: An Historical Review and Present Challenges', in A. Gadd and D. C. Premraj eds., *New Lamps: Fresh Insight into Mission*, published at All Saints', London SW11, 2001, pp 99–116.

6. Cox, Harvey, Fire from Heaven, Cassell, 1996, pp 285–6.
7. Leech, Kenneth, quoting Reuben, A. Sheares II, *The Social God*, Sheldon, 1981, p 92.
8. Crossan, John Dominic, *Jesus: A Revolutionary Biography*, Harper, 1994, pp 90–1.
9. Wink, The Powers That Be, pp 181,197,198.
10. Abbott, Eric Symes, from *Invitation to Prayer*, Forward Movement Publications, 1989, p 83.

8. *The Raising of Jairus's Daughter and the Healing of the Woman with a Haemorrhage*

1. Williams, J., 'Jesus the Jew and Woman', in *Feminine in the Church*, ed. M. Furlong, SPCK, 1984, p 90.
2. Countryman, William, 'The Good News about Women and Men', in *Who Needs Feminism?*, ed. R. Holloway, SPCK, 1991, p 27.
3. Winter, Miriam Therese, in *Woman Word*, Crossroad Publishing, 1990, p 58.
4. Radford Ruether, Rosemary, *Sexism and God-Talk*, SPCK, 1983, pp 136–7.
5. The St Hilda Community, *Women Included: A Book of Services and Prayers*, SPCK, 1991, p 43.
6. The St Hilda Community, *Women Included*, p 44.

9. *The Healing of the Syrophoenician Woman's Daughter*

1. Matthew 8:5–13; Luke 7:1–10.
2. Ewer, W. N., Week-End Book, 1924, p 117.
3. Romans 11:25–26.

10. *The Healing of a Deaf Mute*

1. Matthew 15:29–32.
2. Romans 11:25.
3. Mark 4:11–12.
4. Luke 13:34.
5. Agar, Henry, *A Time for Greatness*, 1942, ch. 7.

6. Donne, John, *Divine Poems, Sermons, Devotions and Prayers,* ed. John Booty, Paulist Press, 1990, p 81.

11. *Three Healings of the Blind*

1. Mark 10:35–45.
2. 2 Corinthians 5:7.
3. Hebrews 11:1.
4. Revelation 3:17–18.
5. Luke 11:34–35.
6. Marshall, Michael, *Pilgrimage and Promise,* Fount, 1981, pp 75–6.
7. Thomas, R. S. 'The Kingdom', in *R. S. Thomas, Collected Poems 1945–1990,* Phoenix Giant, 1995, p 233.

12. *The Healing of a Boy with a Deaf and Dumb Spirit*

1. Exodus 32:1–33:6.
2. E.g. Mark 10:32 and esp. Mark 6:8.
3. Cf. Mark 11:23–24.
4. Ramsey, Michael, *Be Still and Know,* Fount, 1987, p 4.
5. Underhill, Evelyn, 'Life as Prayer', in *The Collected Papers of Evelyn Underhill,* ed. L. Menzies, Longmans, Green & Co., 1946.

13. *The Healing of the Centurion's Servant*

1. Mark 3:22; Matthew 12:24.
2. 1 Corinthians 2:8; Colossians 2:15.
3. Leech, Kenneth, *True God,* Sheldon, 1985, p 321.
4. Theissen, Gerd, *The Shadow of the Galilean,* SCM Press, 1987, p 106.
5. Gillman, Harvey, *A Minority of One,* Quaker Home Service Press, 1988, p 13.
6. Cotter, Jim, extract from Stuart, E., ed., *Daring to Speak Love's Name,* Hamish Hamilton, 1992, p 34.
7. Abbott, Eric Symes, from *Invitation to Prayer,* p 83.
8. The St Hilda Community, *Women Included,* p 80.

14. The Healing of the Man at Beth-Zatha

1. Bruce, F. F., *The Gospel of John*, Eerdmans, 1983, p 121.
2. Bruce, *The Gospel of John*, p 123.
3. According to Deuteronomy 2:14.
4. John 8:11.
5. Mark 3:1–6.
6. Luke 13:10–17.
7. Mark 2:28.
8. John 5:17–18.
9. Dodd, C. H., *The Interpretation of the Fourth Gospel*, Cambridge University Press, 1953, p 320.
10. Matthew 23:23.
11. 'Hell', in Auden, W. H., *A Certain World*, Penguin, 1974.
12. Delft, Stephen, in Kenneth Leech and Brenda Jordan, *Drugs for Young People: Their Use and Misuse*, Pergamon, 1967, p 112.
13. Rowe, Dorothy, *Depression*, Routledge, 1983.
14. Toynbee, Philip, *Part of a Journey*, Collins, 1981, p 13.

15. The Samaritan Lepers

1. Josephus, *The Jewish War* 2:417.
2. Lewis, C. S., *The Four Loves*, Fontana, 1963, p 128.
3. Farrer, Austin, *The Brink of Mystery*, SPCK, 1976, p 68.
4. Herbert, George, *The English Poems of George Herbert*, ed. C. A. Patrides, Dent, 1974, p 135.
5. Underhill, Evelyn, 'Corpus Christi', in *Theophanies*, Dent and Dutton, 1916.

16. The Withered Fig Tree

1. Bundy, W. E., quoted in Nineham, *Saint Mark*, p 299.
2. *Infancy Gospel of Thomas* 3:2.
3. Jeremiah 8:13.
4. Isaiah 5:1–7.
5. Malachi 3:1–3.
6. Zechariah 14:21.
7. Isaiah 56:7.

8. Romans 11:16–24.
9. *Concerning the Jews and their Lies*, 1543.

17. *The Crippled Woman*

1. Mark 3:1–6; Matthew 12:9–14; Luke 6:6–11.
2. Luke 14:1–6.
3. Mark 3:22–30.
4. Luke 13:15.
5. Luke 14:5; Matthew 12:11.
6. Luke 21:28.
7. Mark 7:24–30; Matthew 15:21–28.
8. John 4:7–30.
9. Wink, The Powers That Be, pp 70–1.
10. Galatians 3:28.
11. 1 Corinthians 11:2–16.
12. 1 Corinthians 14:33–36.
13. 1 Timothy 2:8–15.
14. 1 Corinthians 7:21–24; Colossians 3:22–4:1; 1 Peter 2:18–20.
15. Radford Ruether, *Sexism and God-Talk*, pp 33–4.
16. Quoted in *Through the Eyes of a Woman*, ed. W. S. Robins, YWCA, 1986, p 190.
17. Miriam Therese Winter, *Woman Word*, p 77.
18. The St Hilda Community, *Women Included*, p 43.

18. *Two Resurrections*

1. Luke 9:54.
2. Luke 9: 61–62.
3. Luke 4:25–26
4. Luke 10:38.
5. Luke 16:19–31.
6. John 11:35.
7. John 20:6–7.
8. John 11:4.
9. Brown, R. E., *The Gospel According to John*, I, p 432.
10. 1 Corinthians 15:50.
11. 1 Corinthians 15:12; 2 Timothy 2:18.
12. 1 Thessalonians 4:23.

13. John 11:36.
14. Hebrews 5:7.
15. Hebrews 2:17.
16. 'Lazarus to Christ' and 'Christ to Lazarus', David Constantine, *Watching for Dolphins*, Bloodaxe Books, 1983.
17. Winter, Miriam Therese, *Woman Word*, p 55.

19. *Two Miraculous Catches of Fish*

1. Ezekiel 47:9–10.
2. John 12:32.
3. Quoted in R. Lloyd, *The Church of England 1900–1965*, SCM Press, 1966.

Bibliography

This list contains works written about the miracles of Jesus, general works on the historical Jesus, and a number of Gospel commentaries and introductions. Details of other books referred to in the text can be found in the relevant note.

Brown, R. E., *The Gospel According to John*, Chapman, 1984.

Bruce, F. F., *The Gospel of John*, Eerdmans, 1983.

Crossan, J. D., *Jesus: A Revolutionary Biography*, Harper Collins, 1995.

Davies, W. D. and Allison, D. C., *The Gospel According to St Matthew*, T. & T. Clark, 1997.

Evans, C. F., *Saint Luke*, SCM Press, 1990.

Fitzmyer, J. A., *The Gospel According to Luke*, Doubleday, 1981.

Fuller, R. H., *Interpreting the Miracles*, SCM Press, 1966.

Green, B., *The Gospel According to St Matthew*, Oxford University Press, 1975.

Hooker, M., *The Gospel According to St Mark*, Black, 1991.

Luz, U., *The Theology of the Gospel of Matthew*, Cambridge University Press, 1995.

Marshall, C. D., *Faith as a Theme in Mark's Narrative*, Cambridge University Press, 1994.

Meier, J. P., *A Marginal Jew: Rethinking the Historical Jesus*, 2 vols, Doubleday, 1991–94.

Myers, C., *Binding the Strong Man: A Political Reading of Mark's Story of Jesus*, Orbis Books, 1997.

Nineham, D. E., *Saint Mark*, Penguin, 1963.

Richardson, A., *The Miracle Stories of the Gospels*, SCM Press, 1956.

Riches, J., *Matthew*, Sheffield Academic Press, 1996.

Ridderbos, H., *The Gospel of John*, Eerdmans, 1997.

Sanders, E. P., *Jesus and Judaism*, SCM Press, 1985.

—— *The Historical Figure of Jesus*, Penguin, 1993.

Smalley, S., *John*, Paternoster Press, 1998.

Theissen, G., *The Miracle Stories of the Early Christian Tradition*, T. & T. Clark, 1983.

—— *The Shadow of the Galilean*, SCM Press, 1987.

Tuckett, C., *Luke*, Sheffield Academic Press, 1996.

Vermes, G., *Jesus the Jew*, Fontana, 1973.

—— *Jesus and the World of Judaism*, Fortress Press, 1983.

—— *The Changing Faces of Jesus*, Allen Lane, 2000.

Wink, W., *The Powers That Be*, Doubleday, 1998 (This book is a digest of a larger previous work, *Engaging the Powers*, 1992, with elements of two earlier works, *Naming the Powers*, 1984 and *Unmasking the Powers*, 1986 – all published by Fortress Press).

Wright, T., *Jesus and the Victory of God*, SPCK, 1996.